MRS SHAKESPEARE

Robert Nye

MRS SHAKESPEARE

The Complete Works

SOUVENIR PRESS

First published in Great Britain in 1993
by Sinclair-Stevenson, an imprint of
Reed Consumer Books Ltd.

This edition first published 2000 by
Souvenir Press Ltd.,
43 Great Russell Street, London WC1B 3PA

ISBN 0 285 63551 4

Printed in Great Britain by
The Guernsey Press Co. Ltd., Guernsey, Channel Islands

To all good Readers, health
especially
Martin and Janet Seymour-Smith

PART ONE
How Mr Shakespeare
Greeted Me
The Only Time
I Ever Went to London

One
Sweet Mr Shakespeare

"Shall I compare thee to a summer's day?" he enquired politely.

"No thanks!" I said.

You should have seen the look he gave me.

Then he smiled, all white and spiteful.

He smiled at me, Mr Shakespeare, my husband.

Well, I ask you.

Sir Smile, I used to call him.

He wasn't good at much but he was very good at smiling.

That crafty crow, he never laughed a lot.

He never laughed a lot on account of not wanting to show those two black broken teeth he'd got at the front.

He got those rotten teeth from sucking sugar.

Sugarmeats: the man was mad on them.

Gingerbread, marchpane, Naples biscuits.

Sugar was always his poison, right from the start, no doubt because there was so much salt in his blood.

Let me die if I lie.

But he was vain about those bad teeth, I can tell you.

Mr Shakespeare was not in general what I would

call a vain man, not regarding his person, though he could be vain enough about his writing work, and always liked his fellow theatricals to notice how quickly and flowingly he performed it.

You know what they say:

A bee in a cow-turd thinks itself a king.

Marchpane.

Tacky white sicky stuff, like sweet frozen custard with knobs on.

You make it of pounded Jordan almonds and pistachio nuts. A basis of sticky fine sugar, with honey, flour, and essences stirred in.

Sugarplate: that was another one.

That was another of my late husband's favourites.

I remember a Shrove Tuesday at the Sadlers when he got through a whopping great cake of it all on his own.

We just sat and watched him.

He wolfed the whole lot down and then sat there sucking his lips.

That sugarplate of Judith's was gum dragon really, all soaked in rose-water for about two days, then with handfuls of sugar to stiffen it, and the whites of six hen's eggs, plus the juice of two oranges.

Serves four, or was supposed to. Yes, a paste of pure sugar disguised and baked up as a cake.

It was coming out of Mr Shakespeare's ears all Lent.

Hamnet said he must be made of sugar then.

He was a sugarplate creature.

He was a marchpane man.

*

Reader, I speak of my husband, William Shakespeare.

William Shakespeare, of Stratford and London, son of John and Mary Shakespeare (both deceased).

The late Mr William Shakespeare, gentleman, of New Place, Chapel Street, the second biggest house in the whole of Stratford. (And where I'm writing now, if you want to know.)

The same celebrated William Shakespeare who was very famous in his time as the author of 38 plays, 154 sonnets, a complaint of a woman who went wrong, two pornographic narrative poems on classical themes (I'll be coming to them), and a threnody lamenting the death of a pair of chaste birds.

My husband.

Sweet Mr Shakespeare.

The dirty devil.

Talking of birds, you may or may not be aware that some of his poetical admirers call my celebrated other half the Swan of Avon.

I say that's stupid.

I say that simply does not fit the case at all.

Bad ornithology, I call it.

The swan sings when death comes on.

Mr Shakespeare didn't.

He turned his face to the wall and he died a Papist.

When I kissed him then it was like kissing a church candle.

His face burned white.

Rhyme and wine: it's a fatal combination.

Those terrible twins have killed stronger men than him. Yet that was his death-bed.

Am I right?

I am.

But Mr Shakespeare's death-bed is not the subject of my story.

It's another bed I have in mind just now.

It's the best bed I ever saw, or slept in, or made love on.

It's a bed some may say is my dream, and some others a nightmare.

Be that as it may be, your swan is royal. While William Shakespeare was a glover's son.

No silly-sally admirer, but his loving wife and widow all the same, I say he was much more the upstart crow.

I should know, shouldn't I?

That old crow craftiness explains why there's not so many left who would know of his great passion for sucking sugar.

Mr Shakespeare was insatiable, as a matter of fact.

Kissing-comfits, dishes of sugar sops, eringo.

You name it, he ate it – just so long as it was honeyed, candied, sweet.

No sweet without some sweat.

And that's why his teeth went bad and he didn't laugh a lot.

You see, he didn't like people to notice those gravestones he'd got in his mouth as a result of all his sugar-sucking, important people especially, but if you're sly like he was you can smile as much as you want without ever revealing your teeth.

The way Mr Shakespeare did it was he pulled down his top lip when making his smiles, flattening the little hole in the middle which is where my mother once told me the guardian angel leaves the heavenly thumb-print as you come into this world.

May my mother rest in peace, and Sir Smile himself lie easy in Trinity chancel.

Not that I believe in guardian angels.

Not that my husband considered me important.

¶ Two
22 April, 1594

It must have been April the 22nd, the day I'm talking about, and the year would have been 1594.

A feeble sort of a paley-waley day it was.

It was a day unable to make up its mind whether to be spring or to stay winter.

Now of course you will be wondering how I can remember the exact date of a particular day so long ago, and how I can be sure what the weather was like then, and how I can recall just precisely what my husband said to me and I said to him, and so on, and so forth.

I don't blame you.

You might suspect that I'm lying. You might think I'm making it up, or practising fiction.

Well, I'm not.

I tell it as it was, I tell you true.

There will be no fiction here, if I can help it.

I give you my word as I hope to be saved that I shan't be telling you stories.

I happen to be blessed or cursed with a very good memory.

I happen to possess a particularly good memory when it comes to what he said and I said, no doubt because there were years and years when we did not speak to each other at all.

I remember the date of that day because it was the day before St George's Day, which is to say the day before my Mr Shakespeare's birthday and the day before he passed to eternal glory. (Yes, he died on his birthday. He always did like to be neat.)

I remember the weather because I hadn't come dressed for it, and because every little detail of that time is burned into my memory besides, for reasons you'll find out before I'm finished.

I have a strange story to tell you.

Trust me.

It's true what they say:

Truth is stranger than fiction.

(Mr Shakespeare didn't think so? The less Shakespeare he!)

This, then, is what happened.

Listen carefully.

¶ Three
By London Bridge

When Mr William Shakespeare asked me that idle
question as to whether I desired him to compare me to a
summer's day, and I said thank you no, we were standing
together on the bank by London Bridge.

I say together because together is worth remark in
a marriage like ours was.

Himself had been picking his nose for at least five
minutes, dreaming.

As for me, I was counting the heads of the traitors
up there on the poles.

It was cold, I might tell you.

Not a hint of sun in the sky.

Sea-gulls flew over us, squawking.

(Nasty cruel vicious birds, I never liked them.)

"Winter," my husband said suddenly.

He swept off his hat with a flourish, as if he had
just discovered some important new truth.

I thought he'd read my mind about the day not
knowing what season it belonged to.

Then, from the green spark in his eyes, I knew there
was worse to come.

"Winter what?" I demanded.

"Winter you," Mr Shakespeare said. "Anne

Hathawinterway with her," he went on, grinning. "You're more like a day in December," my husband concluded.

I hit him.

Well, what would you have done?

I hit him, though not half as hard as I might have.

It was not like that regrettable occasion when he went head-first into the mill-race at Shottery.

I didn't have a ladle with me in London.

I don't carry kitchen implements about my person.

"Comparisons are odious, sir," I said.

"Did you say odorous?" asked Mr Shakespeare.

I stamped my foot.

I hit him again with my fist.

"Will you call me a bumpkin?" I cried. "Odorous would be bumpkin talk. I did not say odorous."

"Then you must have a head cold," said he.

Some things you can't answer.

What a welcome to London!

What a way to start a holiday!

¶ Four
In Reproof of Poesy

I make no bones about it.

I believe I deserved better treatment.

I think any honest wife or daughter would agree with me.

Consider: I'd come all those miry miles to see him, and I'd made an effort for him.

I mean I was wearing my peachflower taffeta gown with the partlet at the neck, and those new soft green neat's leather ankle-boots.

Mutton dressed up as lamb, as the cruel saying has it, but truly quite presentable mutton.

It was all wasted on him.

God gave him a good woman, but what did he care?

"Wife, shall we admit September to my June?" Mr Shakespeare said.

Go boil your head, I thought.

Think about it.

You just think about it deeply, my dears.

This, you see, is what they call a metaphor.

You take one thing and you say it is another.

It does no good to anybody.

It does nothing for either thing.

You mix up two ideas in the one pretty figure of speech, just to make yourself sound clever.

Clever?

Too clever by half, if you ask me.

Mr Shakespeare, he did it all the time, of course.

You could say it was second nature to him: metaphor.

He got money for doing it, but to my certain knowledge he'd have done it, day in, day out, even if they hadn't been paying him wages for his wit.

He couldn't seem to make the effort and stop himself.

He had wit and to spare, but he didn't always have the wisdom to go with it.

And what he did with words was what he did with his life.

And with his wife.

My husband was a waster.

There, I've said it.

Pardon me for living.

I'll go out into the garden and eat worms.

All the same, since in what I have to say here I'll be trying to tell you the truth as I see it about Mr Shakespeare as well as the truth about me and our marriage and our family and his work and my work and about how it was between us both together and apart in all the years I knew him, you might as well know from the start that I don't think much good ever came anyone's way from poesy's tricks.

That was a long sentence.

I don't like long sentences.

Bv⁺ listen.

What do they do, poets?

(Reader, I married one.)

What do poets do, when it comes down to it?

Poets play around and about with words just to save themselves thinking.

You have to have words to think.

But it's not right or enough just to fool with them.

These metaphors: all they are really are high-class compliments or insults.

One thing cannot be another thing.

It stands to reason.

Thou shalt not commit metaphor, I say.

Especially not in the name of marital sarcasm.

Because, if you must know, I was the eight years older than Mr Shakespeare.

And because Mr Shakespeare never let me forget that small little difference in our ages.

Five
Naples Biscuits

Being as how this book will be about me as well as about my husband William Shakespeare you'll want to know something about me before we go any further.

What can I say?
My name is Mrs Shakespeare.
I was born Anne Hathaway.
I am a widow.
My main subject will be of course my husband.
I call him Mr Shakespeare.
You can too, if you like.

Naples biscuits cost 2s. 6d. a pound.
What a price to pay to feed a sweet tooth!

Six
Gull-Shit

Now then, another bad thing I learned about poesy from knowing my late husband was how easy it is to fall into poesy's trap.

With the very best will in the world, and a devout wish to keep your mind clear, you still feel the pull of it when someone presents you with an image where you wanted a thought.

In those days, that was usually the way with me and Mr Shakespeare.

He'd say something nasty or beautiful and cloud or dazzle my mind's eye with the saying.

The next thing I knew I'd be lost in the world of his language.

It happened most of the time.

It happened now.

I found myself paying him back in the same clipped coinage.

"You flatter yourself with June," I said. "You are August at least."

Then I pulled myself together.

I got a grip on the subject beyond verbal fooling.

"Never mind all that nonsense," I said. "The true

thing, as your mother's always telling me, the true thing is we're only as old as we feel."

And just at that moment, as I invoked his mother's wisdom, a sea-gull went and shat on my husband's head.

It trickled down his eyebrows.

He smiled at me again.

This time there was a sadness in his smile, but it was a sadness out of all proportion to the sea-gull.

As a matter of fact, his look there by the Thames that moment that April day brought back to my mind the way he had smiled at our wedding.

I'd spent years trying to forget that wedding smile.

Some things you can't forget.

He stood shifting from foot to foot in that shaft of winter sunlight in Temple Grafton chapel and he smiled and he smiled, but quite what he was smiling at I could never determine.

I never could bring myself to face that saddest smile of his.

The eyes of Mr Shakespeare were not in it.

It was an empty smile.

It was a smile with the lips only.

It was a smile of the purest lack of meaning.

I returned my own eyes then to the traitors' heads that hung on London Bridge.

"Mothers aren't always wrong," Mr Shakespeare said, sighing. "In which case, I think I shall be coming up to immortality tomorrow."

I daresay that's as clear as mud, isn't it?

Never mind.

I don't know myself what he meant by it exactly.

No doubt it was just his fancy way of saying that he felt he was growing old before his time.

Well, don't we all?

He was wiping his crown and his forehead, and examining his fingers.

I completed my counting.

I like to count when I can.

Counting can be very soothing.

One, two, buckle my shoe.

It helps us on life's way.

One-ery, two-ery, zickary, zan.

Not that I think mathematics is the only thing that counts.

But I finished my counting of those heads then.

"Thirty-two," I said.

My husband glared at me, furious.

"Do you mind, woman? Thirty!"

The next day being, you see, the great man's thirtieth birthday.

"Not your big head," I told him. "Theirs!"

I pointed.

I know, it's rude to point.

But I just couldn't avoid it.

I jabbed my finger at the skulls stuck up on the poles of the bridge.

"You'll find it's thirty-three," said Mr Shakespeare.

I counted them again.

He was right, of course.

His eyes might look half-shut but they never missed much.

A most particular man, was my Mr Shakespeare.

I speak fair where I find it.

I spat on my sleeve then and helped him to clean off the gull-shit.

Seven
Swans

The swans looked grey as old geese on the Thames.

As I hope to be saved, they really did.

I say it myself, but there you have a good comparison.

That comparison strikes me as fair, and solid, and clean of fancy.

Not like his wild talk of comparing a body with a summer's day, or a winter's day or an autumn one for that matter.

Swans are swans, of course, and geese are geese.

Nobody knows that better than I do.

But those London swans that day were bedraggled as geese.

Their backs and necks and feathers were speckled with grime.

Their wings were woebegone.

Their long necks were tucked in against the cold.

They bobbed up and down in the greasy black water, and shivered.

They looked like I felt.

Why, a body with bad eyes (Susanna, for instance) could even have been forgiven for supposing that those poor wretched London swans were geese.

*

Mr Shakespeare stood there combing his thin hair with his fingers.

His hands were like parchment. The light, such as it was, seemed to shine through them.

He had a look in his eyes like the sound of a clump of dirt falling on a coffin.

I noted silently to myself that while he might smile and smile, it was probable that his humour had not been improved by what the gull did.

My husband.

Sour Mr Shakespeare.

The poor shat-upon.

God is no botcher. He makes all parts to fit.

This is a very sad story I have to tell you.

All things considered, it could not be called a nice day. Yet it was as pleasant there where we were as it was anywhere.

Sad is the word to use, though.

Say sad of me and Mr Shakespeare, and you have it.

This is a very sad story.

¶ Eight
Susanna

Susanna is my daughter.

Mine and Mr Shakespeare's.

The first fruit of our union.

The first fruit and the fairest, though a mother ought not to have favourites.

The first fruit and the ripest in wisdom, without doubt.

I love both my dear daughters equally, but Susanna has always been the easier one to love.

She's named after that woman in the Apocrypha, the wife of Joachim, the one falsely accused of adultery by the elders, but Daniel proves her innocence and delivers her, turning the tables on her accusers, and they're put to death instead.

Strange how our given names fit us, isn't it?

"What's in a name?" I always used to say.

Not any more, I can tell you.

Not since that filthy John Lane libel.

But I'll be coming to that.

She's both witty and wise, our Susanna.

She's the cleverest of us who are left behind.

Susanna is presently reading every single one of my

late husband's plays for this folio book of them that some of his theatrical friends are talking of printing in London.

I don't know if that will come to anything, though.

These players are so unreliable.

And would there be many readers for old plays?

Still, it's kind of them to consider such a memorial.

Speaking of which, memorials, last year I helped Susanna arrange for the bust of Mr Shakespeare that a stonemason called Janssen did in Trinity Church.

It was a very fair bust, for a Dutchman.

Some of Mr Shakespeare's London acquaintances came down for the unveiling, and sneered at it, and scoffed out loud in church.

One of them complained that it made Mr Shakespeare look like a prosperous grocer.

But Mr Shakespeare did look like that, in his latter years.

And what's wrong with grocers prospering, I want to know.

Our Susanna says that Mr Shakespeare's plays are full of grief, impiety, and star-crossed lovers.

She tells me that the only happily married couple in all my husband's works are called Macbeth.

Trust him to find his heroes among the heathen.

¶ Nine
My Book

My dear daughter Susanna gave me this book that I'm writing in.

This book was her gift to me last Christmas.

It's a very fine book, and a handsome, bound in ivory-coloured vellum, with a silver clasp with a lock to it, and a little silver key. That key I keep in a locket on a ribbon about my neck.

The title is stamped upon the cover in bold gold letters:

ANNE SHAKESPEARE: HER BOOK.

The pages are creamy and sweet-smelling and smooth to the touch.

The minute I saw it I knew what I'd have to be writing in it.

My story.

His story.

Our story.

The story of the poet, the wife, the best bed, and the bed called second-best.

The true history of how it was between me and Mr Shakespeare.

This silver key will keep that story secret.

I lock my book up when I am not writing.

One day someone will read what I have written, but it won't ever be my daughters or my sons-in-law, nor even my grandchildren, if I can help it.

There are things I must write here which none of my family living should ever have to read.

As God is my judge, truth takes time to blossom.

Truth's a true master, but there's a time and a place for all his lessons, and that time is not yet.

The day after all the immediate members of my family are dead and gone will be soon enough for a reader to be reading this book.

You can see me, though, can't you?

You can see me where I sit here in this dark house, the detested wife, by the light of seven candles placed before my looking-glass to double their flames.

You can see me with the agate ring on my second finger where my pen rests as it scratches in search of meaning across each white page, a woman of quick sense.

You can see my dark eyes.

You can see my dark hair.

But can you see all my darkness yet, O eventual Reader, my friend?

¶ Ten
Writing

Mr Shakespeare liked to write with a goose's quill.

He'd dip it in the ink-pot and his words would wing over the page.

He favoured loose pages, my husband.

He'd write fifty lines on one side, fifty lines on the other.

That way he always knew how much he'd done.

Each page was divided by folding it into four columns.

On the left side Mr Shakespeare would put the name of the speaker, on the right side he'd put the exits and the entrances.

The poesy got written in the middle.

Often I watched him at it, in this very room.

Sometimes, at the end of the day, or in the morning even after a hard night's work, there would be all these loose pages all over the floor, around his feet, while he sat there at his desk, his head upon his arms, he having fallen fast asleep from his exertions.

Poesy must be like that, I suppose. It takes it out of you to write the stuff.

(I have not read his works. I read my Bible.)

My way of writing is the opposite.

I abhor a loose page. I like to write in this compact vellum-bound book. I write tidy, and I write small, and I write slowly.

At the end of a session of such writing I find myself invigorated, not exhausted.

When I had finished writing that chapter last night I looked in my looking-glass, brushing my hair before getting into bed, and my eyes were bright and shining.

My eyes haven't sparkled like that since the day Mr Shakespeare was buried.

That's a hard saying.

But that death-day my eyes were scalded with tears, of course. The more you cry the less you piss, I say.

He smelled faintly of incense.

I felt sick when I kissed him.

I made myself kiss him before John had the coffin nailed down.

It was Quiney who remarked on the way my eyes were burning with their tears.

I kissed him for a last time on the lips.

Dead Mr Shakespeare.

My bad husband.

The darling.

Eleven
The Lavolta

*My dear daughter Susanna could have thought those
swans were geese.*

*She always had bad eyes. She must have been born
with that deficiency.*

I did not discover it until she was four or five.

*Then she came several times running into the house
on Henley Street, crying out "Dada! Dada! Dada!"*

*The poor morsel thought she had seen her father
coming down the road.*

*Alas, it was only her father's father, my
father-in-law John Shakespeare, on his way home from the
alehouse.*

*He'd dance this little dance as he came round the
corner of Meer Street, a dance he had to get danced before
his wife knew his condition. No doubt that dance made
him look younger, which explains my Susanna's mistake.*

Not that she can have seen her father dancing.

Mr William Shakespeare was no dancer.

I once tried to teach him the lavolta.

*The lavolta is easy. It consists in a turn of the body
with two steps, then a high spring, and a pause with the
feet close together.*

Mr Shakespeare fell in the fire.

Not long after mistaking her grandfather for her absent father, Susanna came in and complained of the fog in the yard.

But there wasn't a fog.

It was June, and the day was quite bright.

After that, I found her spectacles.

We bought them at Tiddington Fair.

They cost me three farthings.

She has much more expensive ones these days, rock crystal in frames of thin gold, which her husband had made for her in Bristol.

John calls her his sybil when she wears them.

I write these words with a fine goose-quill once my husband's.

The nib is sharp, the feather is soft to my cheek.

I have a bundle of goose-pens for my future use, and an ink-pot full of black ink of the very best quality. Mr Shakespeare was always fussy about his ink, and he left behind several bottles of iron-gall mixed with green vitriol.

How surprised he would have been to think of his wife finding such good use for it!

I have a splendid sandcaster, too, in the shape of the queen from a chess-set.

Twelve
Dr John Hall

John Hall, my son-in-law, is a medical doctor.

An excellent physician, Dr Hall, and a sound man in matters of religion.

His practice takes him sixty miles about.

He travels on a donkey.

He relieved the Earl of Northampton of a pleurisy, and cured his dropsical countess completely.

I might write more of good John and his medicine chest another time.

My goose-pen does not run to his excellence today.

Today my pen must write of swans like geese. . . .

But what do writers do when they think of something too late?

I expect they go back and change what they have written.

They add, or they subtract.

At all events, they alter what they have said.

I do not think that I can do that here.

For a start, my pages are too creamy.

I don't want blots on them, or crossings-out, or bits between the lines difficult to read.

Besides which, honesty is the best policy (though she

*is not an honest woman who is honest for that reason), and
it seems to me more honest to give you my thinking as it
comes.*

*If I alter or amend then you might think I change
my mind.*

My mind is constant.

I am no chopper, nor no changer.

First words are best words.

*Therefore, if I think of something I have left out,
which it seems to me I should have perhaps put in, then
put it in I shall right when and where I think of it.*

And if that reads rough, forgive me.

*Pardon me, if you please. If not, I, pleased not to
be pardoned, am content.*

This is the way it's going to be in my book.

*This way you can be sure that I'm telling you the
truth as it happens to me.*

*And now why I'm saying this, why I'm burdening
you a touch with my inward deliberations and my credo
of writing-conscience, is because I just this morning
remembered something else about those sea-gulls that
Monday in London in April in the year of Mr
Shakespeare's thirtieth birthday.*

*Yes, may I add now that it is my mature
recollection that those sea-gulls were screaming something
very like a word before one of them saw fit to deliver its
load of white dirt upon my husband's head?*

*"Shakespeare!" those gulls screamed in their
wheeling. "Shakespeare! William Shakespeare!"*

*I just came in from watching two men in the stables
shovelling manure.*

*Steam was rising from the manure and straw
where it was heaped on cold stone between the stalls.*

There was steam too from the men.

They worked with pitchforks.

They pitched forkfuls into a wheelbarrow.

The younger man stood slinging his manure over his shoulder. He was careless, he was confident. He did it with a curt flick of his wrist.

He had gold hair on his wrist.

It looked damp and dark and curly, that gold hair. His eyelashes were dusted with paler flecks of gold.

The manure looked golden too, when he had forked it.

The older man worked carefully, and got more done.

Yes, of course, and I only just now remembered that singular day was a Monday.

¶ Thirteen
Judith

If Susanna is my swan, Judith's my goose.

Judith is my younger daughter.

She was born in 1585, so she's thirty-eight now, two years younger than her sister, though she looks older.

Judith of course is the name of another book in the Apocrypha. She was the heroine who imperilled her own life in the tent of Holofernes, the general of Nebuchadnezzar, in order to save her native town. She cut off that Assyrian's head, and her townsmen, running then on the invaders, defeated them with great slaughter.

The Lord is a man of war (Exodus, 15, iii).

And my Judith is bloody-minded, I will say that.

She needs to be, to be married to that Quiney. A proper waste of space, he is. There are two people I don't like, and he's both of them.

Life has not been easy for my goose Judith.

She is not quick or clever.

She never was a sprag child like Susanna.

Judith was slow and shy and awkward right from the start.

She refused to learn to read or to write her letters. She said she did not ever want to read or to write at all.

"Why not?" I asked her.

"Because I am not my father," Judith said.

I think she meant she did not want to be like her father. Perhaps she thought that reading and writing had taken him away from us to London. For whatever reason, Judith would never learn her ABC, not then, not later. Even now, if she has to witness any document, she simply makes a mark.

Judith did not get married until she was almost thirty-one.

When she did take a husband, she made a disastrous choice.

Thomas Quiney is the black sheep of his family.

His father was Bailiff of Stratford, but the son's a bad lot.

Within a month of his marrying our Judith it came out that he'd already got another local woman pregnant. The woman died in childbirth, and her baby too.

Quiney was sentenced to do public penance in a white sheet for three Sundays in Holy Trinity Church, but he paid five shillings and did private penance instead.

All these events took place in the last weeks of Mr Shakespeare's life.

Susanna says that Quiney business killed him.

She says it broke her father's heart, and killed him.

She said as much to Judith on the day of the funeral.

With the result that Judith did not speak to Susanna for years.

They only spoke again when I told the two of them the truth of it:

That Mr Shakespeare in his last days went back to the drinking of wine.

For years he had held apart from the drunkard's fate.

Then, keeping company with two poet-cronies, he got drunk again, inflaming his brains with fever, and he died.

Whether it was despair at the Quiney business which caused him to drink again, I cannot say.

I think it might have been, don't you?

But for such as Mr Shakespeare that would only be excuse, not reason.

Quiney is now the landlord of a tavern called The Cage, at the corner of Bridge Street and High Street, here in Stratford.

I see him as little as I can.

My obstinate goose girl was born one of twins.

Hamnet and Judith, so we christened them.

They were named for our good friends the Sadlers, their godparents, who I mentioned in my first chapter when I was telling you about my late husband's partiality – well, lust would be more like it – for sugar, candy, sweet things.

Hamnet and Judith Sadler, our friends.

So Hamnet and Judith Shakespeare, our twins.

Only Hamnet died.

Poor Hamnet went to heaven when he was eleven.

Those that God loves do not live long, have you noticed?

Well, anyway, the Sadlers returned our compliment.

When Judith Sadler had a daughter they christened her Anne. And then she had a son and they called him William.

They had fourteen children altogether, our friends the Sadlers, though seven of them died young and two are simple.

Judith Sadler herself's been dead now these nine years.

Hamnet Sadler lives yet, though his baker business down in Church Street was never the same after the great town fire.

Gold is tried in the fire, isn't it?

Hamnet Sadler was a witness to my husband's will, in which he was one of seven old friends left two marks each to buy themselves rings in Mr Shakespeare's memory.

Judith was left just £100 and a silver-gilt bowl by her father's will.

Nine months after marrying Quiney she gave birth to a son.

Shakespeare Quiney, they called him.

But Shakespeare Quiney was not long for this world, and he died aged six months.

The weather's been very cold lately.

The weather's so wonderful cold that all the running rivers round our town are frozen thick.

Tonight I shall make a great fire in the bedroom.

I shall drink a caudle before it, on my green cushion.

I shall take my supper also by the fireside.

This was not a good chapter, but then it is number thirteen.

Fourteen
Twelfth Night

Am I unfair?

Am I lacking all humour to say that Mr Shakespeare was wild in his wanting to compare a body to a summer's day?

Truly as I live and breathe, I don't believe so.

I might be no dancer now, but I danced then.

I know how to laugh.

I was always one for laughing when occasion allowed it.

I know I'm not humourless.

Who laughed the loudest and the longest when Hamnet Sadler wore my old yellow stockings cross-gartered that jolly Twelfth Night?

"Present mirth, present laughter," I always used to say.

All the same, there are limits to humour.

Am I right?

I am.

It was mere fancy, comparing a body to a summer's day.

Fancy dies in the cradle where it lies.

Fancy's all talk and no cider.

I prefer imagination.

There are limits to fancy, but imagination is the king of thought.

Not that I lay claim to imagination.

I don't mean to imply that I do.

Mr Shakespeare was capable of imagination, so I am told, and so I do believe. At his best times, he possessed it, or it possessed him. He released that mighty king in his free mind.

But at other times, when he played with thought, he was fanciful.

I really do believe there's an infinite difference.

At the same time, perhaps I should admit to a certain winter way with me?

But then winter's way is not to be despised.

There's a truth, don't you think, in trees stripped bare of leaves and blossoms?

You see the bone.

You know the skeleton.

And that's the direction we are moving in.

But I know how to laugh before we get there.

So here's a little joke for you, to prove my point:

If he had been deaf and I had been blind we could have been happy.

Fifteen
John Shakespeare's Dunghill

It is here, of course, at my home at New Place, Stratford, that three days ago I watched those two workmen pitchforking manure.

I live here now, with my daughter Susanna and my son-in-law Dr John Hall and their only child, my granddaughter Elizabeth, fifteen and goggle-eyed, sweet as a bee.

That manure will be good for the roses in our knot-garden.

I have seen to it that some is dug also about the roots of the mulberry tree which my late husband planted.

That mulberry tree was his pride and joy.

Like tree, like fruit.

My father-in-law Mr John Shakespeare was once fined by the Stratford elders for keeping a dunghill outside his family house on Henley Street.

Shame in a kindred cannot be avoided.

That was the first indication of what was to go wrong with John Shakespeare's life.

That dunghill in the public way was the first outward and visible sign of the rottenness within.

They fined him one shilling.

Together with his crony, Adrian Quiney, my

father-in-law's drinking companion, also author of a dunghill.

This Adrian Quiney being grandfather to Thomas Quiney, that sinner, now married more's the pity and God save us to my younger daughter Judith, the goose girl, and thus responsible as I have told you for so much of our misery if not for Mr Shakespeare's untimely death.

Bardolfe and Fluellen: they were John Shakespeare's other cronies. All three of them were named recusants in 1592.

When the rainbow touches the tree, no caterpillars will hang on the leaves.

But let me complete this dunghill chapter of my book on a more pleasant note by telling you that New Place is a most commodious house to live in.

It was built over one hundred years ago by the Lord Mayor of London, Sir Hugh Clopton, when he came back to live in his native town.

It has three storeys, five gables, ten fireplaces, and fourteen rooms.

It's a very pretty house of brick and timber, repaired and modelled to my husband Mr Shakespeare's own mind in such matters.

Mr Shakespeare bought New Place for £60.

I made our home here.

And my husband lived here at New Place with me and our daughters for the last part of his life – until his untimely death on his birthday in April 1616, seven years ago to this very day.

Sixteen
Stratford Spring

It's that other April day I remember now. It's that earlier April of 1594 that I want you to picture in your mind's eye. It's the year of Mr Shakespeare's thirtieth birthday. It's the year I went to London for the first and only time.

As I think I told you before, it was a wishy-washy sort of a day for April, that day I came there.

No sap in it.

No sinew.

Not like real spring at all.

I'd left the spring behind me in Stratford the week before, a spring in such a rush that the hawthorn had been out before the blackthorn was over.

There was a spring.

That was Stratford spring.

Like that first spring I knew him, almost, when we went a-maying.

He carried my shoes and I drew my gown through the pocket-hole of my petticoat and I danced in my smock in the dew.

We went down by Clopton Dingle.

We came back by Snitterfield Bushes.

And we stopped in the Ingon meadows.

I sang to the tunes of the birds and the brooks.

I washed my face in the long grasses.
I wore that wild thyme in my hair.
He plucked me the twigs of the catkin.
He crowned me his Queen of the May.
And the maypole at Marston was tall as a giant,
that first spring I knew Mr Shakespeare.

One thing you must never do when you go a-maying.
You must never let a single blossom of the hawthorn
fall inside the house.
If you do, it means death.
If you do, it brings a death in the house.
Wild thyme and sprigs of rosemary go within, to
keep the air sweet and clean from all infection.
Hawthorn is only for garnishing every door and
window.
You hang hawthorn over the threshold, and round
every doorpost.
But never, never, never bring the hawthorn in.
Didn't his own sister Anne die under the wreath
that she'd crowned herself with, when he was a boy of
ten?

Lady-smocks and crow-flowers bloomed in the Snitterfield
meadows. Marigolds too. Marybuds, I called them.
Rank frumiter grew in the hedgerows by Ingon,
their flowers waxy red where they were not yellow.
We were very young.
We were merry as magpies.

That maypole at Marston was high as the mast on Sir
Francis Drake's ship, so they said.
There were long wreaths of flowers that hung down
from it, and ribbons, and streamers.

The men and women danced in rings about the whole day long.

The mere sight of that maypole gave a glow to my heart, and spread a charm for me across the country round.

Praise the Lord, but I know better now.

And the Lord knows there was nothing like that in London that cruel April day when the swans looked grey as old geese on the Thames.

Not a maypole in sight.

Not a mayer.

We were a week away from May Day, I grant you that.

But when May Day came, no maypole would come with it.

London: no maypoles.

Just those thirty-three heads of traitors and heretics stuck on poles on London Bridge.

And the great roar of the river through the arches.

Twenty arches.

London Bridge has twenty arches.

I should know.

I counted them.

Well, it was something to do.

You have to have something to do.

I had finished helping my husband Mr Shakespeare clean the gull-shit from his person.

He had thanked me kindly.

I had assured him to think nothing of it.

As one does.

But then he did.

I mean, think nothing of it.

Now he just stood there smiling his complicated

smile for no good reason that I could see, and humming to himself.

Now I just stood there, not smiling, not humming, for every good reason in the world that a wife might have.

Sir Smile ignored me.

I might as well have been a bit of gull-shit.

He would perhaps have paid me more attention if I had been a bit of gull-shit.

Well, I wasn't having that.

So I developed this very close interest in the scenery, such as it was.

I counted the houses on London Bridge. (I forget how many.)

I counted the number of arches between the bank where we stood and the drawbridge that let the tall ships through. (Thirteen.)

But when I had finished counting all the arches in London Bridge I began to hate London.

I began to wish that its bridge would fall down with a clatter in the dirty river Thames.

I began to wish that I'd stayed at home in Stratford.

Seventeen
Unreal City

If you want to know, London struck me as about the coldest place I ever was.

A cold place and a dirty, London town.

The people smelled.

I make no bones about it.

The people smelled but they were grey ghosts all the same.

An unreal city, London. A make-believe place.

I'd say it was like a playhouse, but then I have never set foot in a playhouse in my life.

So I'd better just say it was as I would imagine a playhouse if I had to: a place with no soul, a place where smelly ghosts strut up and down.

I saw a boy with a ragged woollen cap picking pockets.

Nobody seemed to notice what he did.

I saw rag-pickers with put-on woeful faces, who had managed their sores and their ulcers so as to try to move compassion.

I saw strollers and posture-masters, and milliners and puppet-men, and fiddlers and toy-women.

All of them looked as if they mocked at religion and at death.

I saw a city of the dead.
A place of shadows.
Like a beast with many heads and no true heart.
Let me die if I lie.
It was all unreality, London.
I began to wonder if I was really there.
But I was really there. It was London that wasn't.
Even the breeze coming chill off the river that late afternoon was like no wind that I would care to call a real wind.

That breeze was no wind like the wind in Arden Woods or up on Stinchcombe Hill.

That London breeze was just a swirling smoky stench of bad-cooked cabbage and garbage.

It stuck in my throat.
It made me feel sulky and sick.

London is a living graveyard, I say.
London is where all the dead people live.

¶ Eighteen
Whores and Apple-Squires

My mother used to tell me that London was for whores.

"London women are whores," she said. "London men are apple-squires."

I looked up and down but I saw no whores in London.

I saw beggars with their clackdishes.

I saw shawled women with babies with purple eyelids.

I saw bullies for little lords. They marched along clearing the way with their canes and their cudgels.

I saw poor folk pushing, and begging for alms, and shouting their wares.

I saw a priest spit.

I heard a proud lady fart.

I saw black-fronted taverns, with doorways so squat you would have thought that only dwarfs could get into or out of them.

I saw the latest crab-shell coaches.

I saw and heard a world that was running nowhere on noisy wheels.

But, to be honest, there was never a whore in sight.

All the same, I think I know what my mother meant, and I do believe she was right.

*

Apple-squires: I never understood that.

I asked Mr Shakespeare once, but he would not explain it.

He went red in the face when I asked him, but he would not explain it.

That sinner Quiney happened to overhear our conversation (it was when he first came hanging about the house in quest of Judith, and I'd asked Mr Shakespeare the question out in the orchard). Later, grinning, Quiney told me an apple-squire was a pimp.

But I think it is worse.

No, friends, they can keep their rat-packed flea-picked London as far as I'm concerned, and what my late lamented husband ever saw in its maggots I honestly couldn't explain for you.

Except, of course, the playhouses.

I know that in those days he had to be near the playhouses for his trade.

Every man must walk in his trade.

Also, confess it I must, there was Mr Shakespeare's liking for the lordly ones. From the time when Julius Caesar built the Tower of London and put the lions in it, there have always been more great and lordly ones in London than in other parts, so ambitious men have gone there to be near them.

But then great ones are not good ones more than others.

Nor are lordly ones more than other people true ones.

I could have told him that if he'd stayed at home.

Good ones are true ones and sometimes it is easier for humble ones to be good ones than for great ones to be anything but shadows.

I could have told him that, too.

Ask questions at your hearth, the place of answers.

The playhouse is a palace of shadows.

And London is a kingdom of playhouses.

And what if humble country ones can be good ones and true ones more often and more easily than the great and lordly city ones can be anything but shadows?

Notice, I do not say that city ones are bad ones.

Nor that the lordly is always the evil.

That would be simple-minded.

But I do say that my mother had a point about those whores.

My mother was long dead when I came to marry.

My father died a year before that day, bequeathing me ten marks to be paid upon it.

£16 13s. 4d.

That was my marriage portion.

Nineteen
Lions

If Julius Caesar built the Tower of London?

Did Julius Caesar build the Tower of London?

Mr Shakespeare said he did, but I beg leave to doubt it.

I don't believe everything that Mr Shakespeare told me.

I was not born yesterday.

However, there are lions in the Tower of London.

I did not see them.

But I heard them roar.

I like the idea of lions.

Dr John Hall tells me the lion is an emblem of the Resurrection.

The lion's whelp is born dead, and remains dead for three days, until the father lion breathes on it and it receives life.

My good son-in-law tells me also that Mark the Evangelist is symbolised by the lion, because he begins his gospel with the scenes of John the Baptist and Jesus in the wilderness.

They say that if you can wrap your clothes in a lion's skin it will kill the moths.

They say that lion-meat will cure bad dreams and fantasies in the night-time.

They say that the gall of a lion being taken in drink by anyone will kill or poison him out of hand.

And I read it in Purchas' Pilgrims that the lioness, by showing her hinder parts to the male, can make him run away.

And that so great is the fear of lions to wolves, that if any part of a lion's grease is cast into a fountain, the wolves will never dare to come and drink from it.

For these and other reasons I like lions.

The wicked flee when no man pursueth: but the righteous are bold as a lion (Proverbs, 28, i).

The lion will not touch the true prince.

(Even John Shakespeare said that, in his cups.)

Mr Shakespeare should have taken me to see the lions in the Tower of London.

Twenty
Endearments

I was shivering.

My teeth started chattering.

Mr Shakespeare took off his cloak and wrapped it around my shoulders.

"Cheer up, little autumn," he said to me.

Calling me autumn was the nearest he had got to affection since I had arrived.

He never overflowed with endearments, not in my case.

Calling me little was simply accurate.

I'm five feet one and a quarter inches in my stocking feet.

Mr Shakespeare was all of six foot.

When he stood up straight, that is.

When he took trouble to unfold himself.

He had the stoop of a clerk.

It was all that scribbling bent his spine, no question.

He was very thin, also, in those days.

If you'd looked at him sideways, you wouldn't have seen him.

I'm sorry. I don't mince my words.

You can take it or leave it.

But Mr Shakespeare was tall, that I grant you.

I had to look up to him.

I looked up to him then.

"Is it very far to go, dear?" I asked timidly.

I might have been enquiring the way to Babylon.

I was cast down quite, and overwhelmed by London.

I wanted a hot meal.

Hot spicy ribs of beef would just have suited me.

Or a red-deer pie with gravy and green beans.

I wasn't going to get either, I could tell that.

I wasn't going to get any real meal at all.

Already I could see that it was going to be one of those days.

Little did I know that it was going to be followed by a night like no other night in my whole life.

"I'm still cold," I told my husband. "How far is it?"

"Bishopsgate," said Mr Shakespeare. "Just by St Helen's. It's not all that far. And the walking will warm you, won't it?"

He hesitated, awkward, twisting his hat in his hands, biting his lip as he always did before touching me.

Whenever I saw my husband bite his lower lip I could always expect him to touch me.

We stood there staring at each other for a long moment.

The river roared under the arches.

Ghost people milled about us.

A church bell tolled the hour: six o'clock.

I nodded.

Mr Shakespeare said: "Let us go then."

He took my arm and we set forth together for his lodgings.

PART TWO
The Walk
Across London

Twenty-One
The Cloak

It was a very fine cloak that Mr Shakespeare had wrapped about my shoulders.

It was made of brocaded velvet.

It was tawny in colour.

There was this palest pink silk in the lining, very smooth and cool and pleasing to the touch.

I stroked that lining with my fingertips as we walked along.

It felt as soft as swansdown.

This splendid cloak was cut in the Italian style.

It swirled to my step.

Don't think that I am ignorant of fashion just because nearly every day of my life has been passed here at Stratford.

I know a hawk from a handsaw.

And I know a well-cut cloak when I see one.

I know what cut is Italian, what English, what French.

That tawny velvet cloak of Mr Shakespeare's was perhaps the best cloak I ever saw, save in the Queen's pageant at Kenilworth.

Let me die if I lie.

Without doubt that cloak of Mr Shakespeare's was the very best cloak I ever wore.

As we walked along together I had the chance to take note of the rest of my husband's apparel.

Now that the cloak was off him I could see what he looked like unwrapped.

And he made quite an eyeful!

Mr Shakespeare was wearing a black silken doublet, well-padded in the chest but hollow-bellied below, with close-set silver buttons winking down the front.

This doublet went with a starched white cartwheel ruff and foamy lace wrist-ruffs.

There was also a decorated codpiece the colour of burnished copper.

Mr Shakespeare's silk hose were paned with canions.

He wore a copotain hat on his head.

This was the hat he had taken off with a flourish when he bethought himself rather to compare me to a day in winter.

If he had left the hat on, it wouldn't have mattered about the gull-shit.

That served him right, no doubt.

But the hat was a mistake.

I hated that hat.

Hats never suited Mr Shakespeare.

I remember the hat he wore to our Susanna's wedding.

It looked like a stovepipe growing out of his skull.

The wind blew it off, and he got cross because no one would chase after it.

What did he expect? We had our own finery to take care of.

Mr Shakespeare was never what you might call a runner.

And by then his leg was lame, what with the gout in it.

Lame dogs should not wear hats to their daughters' weddings.

Especially not when the wind is north-north-west.

Let's face it, Readers:

Sir Smile was simply not a hat person.

His head was too big for any hat to sit there happily for long.

Hats perched atop his skull like pigeons on a monument, just waiting for an excuse to fly away.

Still, although I didn't like it, this copotain hat of my husband's looked another expensive item to my eye.

It had evidently been chosen with some care to go with the cloak.

The crown of the hat was tawny, the underbrim pink.

A peacock's feather was fastened to the side of it with a gold-plated buckle.

This outfit of Mr Shakespeare's must have cost a pretty packet, I reckoned.

And I'm talking, remember, about the last decade of last century, when a pair of kersey socks could set you back three shillings and velvet never came at less than a pound a yard.

O the cost of clothes in those days.

I remember when Hamnet lay dying and he wanted the newfangled boots.

They were what they called lugged boots, hanging loose about the leg, turned down and fringed.

They cost me seven shillings and fourpence halfpenny.

Hamnet wore them lying on his bed, but never to walk.

We buried him in those lugged boots of his.

"Peas porridge," Mr Shakespeare said suddenly.

"I beg your pardon, sir?" I said.

"That cloak," Mr Shakespeare said. "They call the colour peas porridge."

It seemed to me a cheap apology for extravagance:
To give such a homely name to so splendid a thing.

¶ Twenty-Two
A Piece of White Cloud

I said nothing to my husband about the cloak.

I wore it with pleasure.

I dabbled my fingers in its silk lining, and folded it this way and that as we walked along.

I held it slantwise like a veil across my face when bullies stared at me, or chapmen came leapfrogging out of shop doorways, or horses' hoofs kicked mud up from the street.

I made that peas porridge velvet ripple and billow to my stride.

But I did not care to comment on the excellence of the cloak, nor the hat, nor the hose, nor the doublet.

You see, Mr Shakespeare had not exactly been sending sackfuls of rose nobles or gold jacobuses via the carrier home to Stratford for the housekeeping.

For years I had been living on very little more than a diet of promises.

Seven lean years.

How I managed was by living with his parents.

How I survived was by scrimping. (Waste not, want not.)

I relied on John and Mary Shakespeare, and that was not good.

That house in Henley Street was not a happy home.

I did my share with the care of it, and the cooking and the cleaning, but my bed there was always uneasy.

Uneasy and uncomfortable, with a stinging nettle in it.

They thought their eldest son had married too young, that I had trapped him.

Mary Shakespeare loved her grandchildren, and I believe she grew to love me a little after her husband's death left her free to have a heart again.

But in those days, between old Mr Shakespeare's going soreheaded to the alehouse and his coming home drunk, she seemed to have time only for holding me in some way responsible for my own Mr Shakespeare's absence.

"If it wasn't for you," she said once, "he'd have stayed at home in Stratford like other men."

I never understood this.

Unless she meant my tongue?

My tongue is well hung, that I grant you.

But it never yet cost me my head.

My mother-in-law, shall we say, considered me a shrew.

For my part, I considered her a saint.

(Not that I have need of saints in my prayers, you understand.)

All I mean to say is that Mary was certainly saintly in what she put up with from my father-in-law, and from Mr Shakespeare too in his younger days.

I'll be coming to that.

He followed his father in sin like a little curtal dog.

As for John Shakespeare: despite all, I can recall him with affection.

He was the fellow with the great belly, a merry-cheeked old man.

He had been by trade a glover, but he was also a dealer in wool, a money-lender, and a trader in barley and timber, sheep, skins, meat and leather.

Wine was his doing and his undoing.

He used it at first no doubt as many do – as an aid to affability, as oil in his business dealings which were often undertaken in the taverns.

But the day soon came when he could not do any business without his wine-jug.

And then came many more days when the wine and not the business was his all.

When those days came, John Shakespeare became a drunkard.

He lived to drink. He had no other life.

For the drunkard and the glutton shall come to poverty: and drowsiness shall clothe a man with rags (<u>Proverbs</u>, 23, xxi).

My husband was removed early from the grammar school as a consequence of his father's downfall and disgrace.

John Shakespeare's whole life was lived and wasted in the shadow of the vine, and yet (as I say) it was not always ugly, or lacking love.

Sometimes even when he was drunk a rare sweetness would possess him. He seemed almost to become it.

His wife shared this with him, although she never drank.

It existed between them. It took both of them.

It was a something childish, but very natural.

I remember once when he was drunk on Christmas

Eve on sherris sack, and he asked the two of us for a piece of white cloud.

His eyes filled with tears and he begged the two of us for a piece of white cloud.

It was what he wanted for his Christmas gift, he said, because it was impossible.

I did not know what to do or what to say, but Mary just told him to wait a moment.

Then she went out into the garden and gathered a handful of new-fallen snow for him.

When she gave old John Shakespeare that handful of snow he stopped crying, and kissed it.

He fell asleep with that handful of snow pressed to his lips.

He was sleeping like a child before it melted.

But once I saw John Shakespeare kick his wife downstairs.

And more than once he put his hands on me.

Henley Street was not paradise, I can tell you.

I lived there for seven lean years on my father-in-law's charity.

It was not as I liked it, I must admit.

But at least I never begged or borrowed, stole, or starved.

Susanna says that the matter of drink and drunkenness is explored by my husband in a number of his plays — especially in Antony and Cleopatra, 2, vii, and The Tempest, 2, ii, and in the second part of King Henry VI, 2, iv, but that the key passage in which Mr Shakespeare gives away his knowledge of the hellish power wine holds over some souls comes when he has his character Hamlet turn aside before encountering his father's ghost to make a *long speech on that subject which has nothing to do with the play.*

Susanna says that this Hamlet play is my husband's longest, but that it is full of stuff which he does not make sense of. She says that we must simply admit that here Mr Shakespeare tackled a problem which proved too much for him. To understand it, in Susanna's opinion, we should have to understand things which he did not understand himself.

I say this may be too kind to her father.

But then a wife may tell some truths which a daughter cannot.

The wife is the key to the house.

I say he knew what poisons life and obstructs action.

My husband.

Sad Mr Shakespeare.

His father's son.

Twenty-Three
Secrets

He would soon make his fortune, Mr Shakespeare said.

I mean when he first left me and the children and ran off to London.

That would have been the Easter the back chimney caught fire.

Which is to say (to make it nice and historical) the year before the year of the great Armada.

Our Susanna was not quite four.

The twins were just two.

Mr Shakespeare was twenty-three, in the prime of his prematurity.

O but he was burning with ambition.

His hair came flying out in handfuls when he talked of what he wanted to do.

He would tug at it as he talked, his eyes ablaze.

He was all talk, all aspiration, all desire for the world of men.

Why, he was jealous of the sun, in my estimate.

His lips did not taste of tears as he bade me goodbye.

"I'll write," he promised.

(And I thought he meant letters!)

"Great prospects, wife," he said. "A sea voyage with Sir Francis Drake, no less."

Well, I can't believe that he had any hand in the scattering or the sinking of Spain's Armada. . . . He never could abide the sight of blood. When I cut my thumb chopping onions, he keeled over fainting.

Later there was report of another sea voyage, was there not?

To a place called Aleppo.

In a vessel called The Tiger.

Such a shame that some shipwreck off the sea-coast of Bohemia left our bold young mariner penniless again.

Did my husband ever go to sea a sailor?

I couldn't tell you.

I can tell you that Bohemia has no sea-coast.

And that Aleppo, which is in Turkey, is not a port. (I looked it up.)

I don't know what he was doing in those earliest days away, to tell you the truth.

Sir Smile was always a slyboots.

He liked to tell lies for the hell of it, that I am sure.

By hell I mean sport.

To a devil, confusion is amusement.

But there's more to this matter than that.

Mr Shakespeare told lies not just for hell's sake.

Mr Shakespeare thought that lying confirmed him in his soul's freedom.

He would not be pinned down by facts.

He never could abide you to fix him.

So, for as long as I knew him, Mr Shakespeare used his fancy to make stories about himself that kept him free.

It was second nature to him.

And it gave him, in his own eyes, a second life.

For example: If he had been to Wilmcote he would say he'd been to Bidford.

Not because he'd done anything wrong at Wilmcote necessarily, nor for any reason at all, save the reason that he did not want you to know where he had been.

At such moments you would see *his* eyes enjoying your innocent belief that he had passed the day in Bidford.

He liked to see you thinking of him walking down that lane, seeing those chickens, speaking with this woman or that man.

While in his heart he knew it had been otherwise.

Since in his heart he knew that he'd been in Wilmcote, seen other creatures, gone down different ways, spoken with persons you were not thinking of.

By such means Mr Shakespeare kept his true life secret.

Not for any good reason.

Just because that was the way with him.

Similarly, I suppose, it was the wrong road always that drew his feet.

If you told him that at Wilmcote he would see the maypole, then he would thank you and seem glad and interested but when you had gone he would take the road for Bidford.

Did Mr Shakespeare think that his dream of the maypole must always be more perfect than the dance?

Or did he take the wrong road because he belonged on the wrong road, by reason of its wrongness, which matched his own?

It was Hamnet and Judith who wanted me to have seen those lions in the Tower of London.

When I came home they begged me to tell them about them.

What were their manes like? Did they eat honey?
What were their paws like? Their claws like? And so on
and so on.

I could not lie to them.

I told my little ones that I had heard the lions,
that's all.

And did I care? Did I care that Mr Shakespeare had his
secrets?

Reader, I cared for him.

And so I did not care about them at all.

Not about the secrets, not about his little white
lies.

I knew my husband well. I knew the look that spoke
of Bidford when its face had been to Wilmcote.

I knew that face's lord and owner just couldn't help
it.

The having to be free to make words mask the truth
of him.

So after a while I asked Mr Shakespeare no
questions.

And he told me no more lies about Aleppo.

Nor spoke again of having been to sea a sailor.

Especially not after that afternoon the cockle boat
sank on the Avon when he was home visiting and taking
our Susanna and the twins for a row downriver.

They ran over the weir.

They very nearly drowned.

It was the Alveston millkeeper had to fish them all
out with his hook.

Well then, here we are ending a chapter of my story going
through the streets of hell (or London), with me in the
expensive peas porridge cloak, and my husband beside me

in clothes that must have cost a twelvemonth's housekeeping.

And I hope by now you understand how it was that Mr Shakespeare had to have his secrets.

Not that I am so vain or so foolish as to think I have explained it.

The human heart's a mystery, thank God.

And only God in his infinite wisdom will ever know the ends of it.

Yet I hope that what I have said serves to put you in the picture as to how it was with Mr Shakespeare's version of that part.

I mean the heart.

He was not free at all.

He was fancy's prisoner.

As you will learn, this book of mine is about the biggest of Mr Shakespeare's little secrets.

All the time we are moving towards it.

You'll find that secret out, if you stay with me.

I was a part of it.

I was my husband's accomplice.

You wait.

You'll see.

Do I make him out too artful a man altogether?

Perhaps I do. And that is a fault, if I do.

He had his simple moments, Mr Shakespeare.

Why, once, in the early days, he gave me a white rose with a kiss, and called me his angel.

But women are not angels, though they have angels' faces.

And, as for me, my face was never angel-like.

*

Now I open my big mouth and the truth falls out:
Mr Shakespeare was always as full of secrets as a
cow's tail is of burrs.

¶ Twenty-Four
Horse-Wife

Not to mince matters, let me tell you this:

I sent my brothers after him.

I sent them by the Banbury road to London to visit our fortune-maker.

The first time they went they found out and brought me back word that Mr Shakespeare had employment all right.

My husband was a horse-wife!

They told me you could find him any night at the door of the playhouse, in waiting.

His job there was holding the horses.

Gentlemen might ride to the play without servants in attendance.

What could such gentlemen do with their horses while they were in the playhouse?

Answer: Mr Shakespeare would hold them.

That can't have paid much.

All the same, it would have started to pay better once he got the trade organised.

My brothers reported he had done this, the second time they went.

Now Mr Shakespeare was no longer holding horses.

Now he was employing boys to hold the horses for him.

They worked under his direction, this team of ostlers.

They advertised him, too.

When a gentleman dismounted, calling out "William Shakespeare!" to summon the reliable horse-minder, one of my husband's minions would spring forward, cap in hand, shouting:

"I am Shakespeare's boy, sir!"

This name of <u>*Shakespeare's Boys*</u> *was soon given to all such playhouse horse-wives, my brothers said.*

I only ever wrote one letter to Mr Shakespeare. It read as follows:

> *"Dear Husband, – This is just to tell you that I love you, supposing you should have forgotten it by the time you get to London.*
>
> *Your poor, but unscrupulously honest,*
>
> *Anne."*

Twenty-Five
Keeping Chicks

By the next time I saw Mr Shakespeare himself, he had worked his way up from the horses.

He had progressed from the outside to the inside of the playhouse.

That must have been when he came home for the twins' fourth birthday, the February of 1589.

He told me, when I asked him, that now he was a thing called a prompter's assistant.

Or was it an assistant prompter he said he was?

And, in any case, because I think he said a prompter's assistant, shouldn't I suspect that he was really in all probability an assistant prompter?

(See Chapter Twenty-Three.)

(See his whole life.)

Be that as it may.

Mr Shakespeare had his foot inside the playhouse.

Though I confess it escapes my memory whether this first inside-the-playhouse employment of my husband and his foot was as a prompter's assistant or an assistant prompter.

It was better than being a horse-wife, I do remember that.

It involved shouting at the actors, I remember that also.

Mr Shakespeare told me he had to call to the actors to go on the stage.

He told me some of his other important prompting and assisting duties, but I'm sorry to say I have forgotten what they were.

Never mind. I do remember the main thing.

The main thing was the prompter's assistant's pay.

You couldn't have kept chicks on it.

I should know, shouldn't I?

I had to try.

And we had three of them.

I say money deserves and must have its own paragraph in this book.

Money.

Like that.

Twenty-Six
Under the Crab Tree

It takes two to make a quarrel.

Sometimes I've wondered if Mr Shakespeare would have stayed at home with me in Stratford if I had not had twins.

It must have been quite a blow for him, as well as a joy, when I had them.

What if we had only had Susanna?

Susanna of course we had to have, my dear wise bespectacled swan.

We might not have had each other without our Susanna.

I mean he might never have married me if she had not been on the way.

But then, and just two months before his own twenty-first birthday, there Mr Shakespeare was suddenly saddled with a wife and three children.

Don't think I am daft, or hard-hearted.

Don't imagine I have not tried often enough to see these situations as he must have seen them.

He never spoke about it directly to me.

He never much complained, or regretted, or scolded.

But perhaps that fourfold burden was too much for him?

Especially there in two rooms in Henley Street.

I know there were times when both of us found it hard to think straight in Henley Street.

What with John Shakespeare's drinking.

What with Mary Shakespeare's saintly fuss.

But listen.

There was another reason for his going.

Mr Shakespeare was running away from what he knew he might become if he remained.

Tell the truth and shame the devil.

Tell it I shall, though it shame others besides the devil.

Tell it I must, though it shame him and me as well.

Mr Shakespeare drank deep and hard himself in those long-ago days.

For a spell he sank down in the same drunken sty as his father.

They'd roister and swagger and jest together, the fat red-cheeked old man and the young one as thin as a stick.

Father and son, what a scandal!

Grey beard and no beard both drowning in tubfuls of ale!

That did not last long.

It finished the night when the two of them, father and son, slept under the crab tree.

It rained.

They lay there in each other's arms till dawn.

They had got so drunk that they could not even crawl home.

Next day, when my husband fell in through the door, he said nothing about it.

He lay for three days on his bed, with his face to the wall.

When the old man came to him, he would not go again with him to the alehouse.

He would not speak a word to his father. He ignored him. He turned his head away.

He just lay there on the bed, not sleeping, not waking, staring at the wall.

When Mr Shakespeare got up, he went away to London.

Going to London, he left his father and his father's ways behind him.

Going away, he quit his own wild youth.

Mr Shakespeare had to leave such things behind.

Alas, for I was left behind as well.

I believe that in London Mr Shakespeare was no drunkard.

Some of the other playmakers were dissipated men, great frequenters of taverns, but he kept himself apart.

If they came knocking on his door and requesting his company in their carousings my husband used to say that he was in pain and could not.

How I wish he'd done that after Judith's wedding!

Wine is the soul's destroyer.

The more the wine-drunk man drinks, the more he is athirst, like a worm that sucks blood.

Twenty-Seven
Sherris Sack

His father went on drinking when he was gone.

If anything, the wretched old man drank even more swinishly after.

He went from bad to worse, then worse, then worst.

I saw it all. I was there in Henley Street.

John Shakespeare, a tenant farmer's son, had risen high by his own labours.

John Shakespeare had been in his prime the Chief Alderman of Stratford.

He'd been Constable and Chamberlain and Bailiff of our town before he held that office.

This man, who had climbed so high, fell lower than those born slaves, and all as a result of the one beastly imperfection.

He ended as a sot.

A slave to drunkenness.

He neglected his business, then abandoned it.

He failed so often to attend the Council meetings that finally they lost patience and threw him out.

He sank deeper and deeper into debt then.

He mortgaged his wife's inherited lands and lost them. (This broke her heart, though she still prayed for him.)

All his good qualities sank like lead down to the bottom of his carousing cups.

He became just a clay-brained guts, just a huge hill of flesh.

He went about wearing an old ragged doublet and a torn pair of breeches, with his hose out at his heels, and a pair of old broken slip shoes on his feet, a rope about his middle instead of a girdle, and on his head an old greasy cap which had so many holes in it that his hair started through it.

Soon all that he owned was the house and the shirt on his back.

And half the house and all the shirt would be owing to the innkeepers.

In the last years of his life, John Shakespeare did not even dare to go to church for fear of being served with a process for debt.

He'd sit hunched by the fire downing sherris sack all day.

That was always his drink.

Sherris sack.

A rough white wine, which the old man drank brewed, or mulled, or burnt, or with sugar and perhaps a toast in it, or eggs.

He lived on this sack, when he'd passed the need for food.

He still told his jokes and his stories, but nobody was listening.

He ended obscene and greasy, gross as a mountain, lying on his back on a bed that had broken with the weight of him.

His life that had been all riot turned all remorse.

John Shakespeare became a Papist.

Then he died.

Twenty-Eight
Third Murderers

Enough of such horrors.
Back to my own lean years. . . .

It must have been through the assistant prompting that my husband got in now with Mr Burbage.

I mean Mr James Burbage, the manager, a good man of business.

And it must have been about then, when he first got in with Mr Burbage, that Mr Shakespeare did a spell of acting on stage.

Now you might fancy that what with all the little lies and pretences about Bidford when he'd really been to Wilmcote, you might suppose that the great pretender would have proved to be a good actor.

Well, he didn't.

Not so I have heard.

And from sound judges too, as a matter of fact.

I mean from such as saw and heard him at it.

His youngest brother Ned, for instance.

Quite a talented actor, they said Ned was. And he must have been. I believe he even acted in my husband's plays. That my husband wrote some parts especially for him. Rosalind, one of them was called, so I remember. (Men have to pretend to be women there in the playhouse.)

Young Ned said his brother Will did not act very well.

I'm not surprised really.

Mr Shakespeare may have been an accomplished liar, but God never cut him out for the acting trade.

Private lies, yes.

Public acts, I think not.

He lacked what they call Stage Presence and his voice had no variety.

So Ned said.

Edmund, he had this Stage Presence. And his voice could sing and speak both high and low.

Mr William Shakespeare, on the other hand, got stuck with what his brother called the minor parts.

Ghosts, heralds, third murderers, fourth messengers, and so forth.

And even in those parts he had no success.

He would forget his lines and have to make up his own speeches on the spot.

But this gave Mr Burbage a great notion.

He set his failed actor to work patching up other men's plays, taking stale stuff and resurrecting it, breathing new life on old bones.

The breakthrough at last, my husband said.

He was pleased. He was as pleased as Punch.

His Judy didn't quite know what to think.

(And doesn't still. The world is not a stage.)

But, for a brief bright interval, things went swimmingly.

Mr Shakespeare could work very fast when he wanted to.

It was always like that. Once he weeded the garden

for me in half an hour. He pulled up all my moonwort and hart's tongue and naked nannies, but he certainly got rid of every weed as well.

In London then, working for Mr Burbage on those old plays, he worked fast and he worked hard and he worked long.

That Christmas of 1590, when the Charlecote pond froze over, he sent gifts home by the carrier for all of us.

I got garters of best silk of Granado.

He sent this doll for Susanna, with arms and legs that moved, and eyes that closed.

And a musical box for Hamnet and Judith, our twins.

Judith's still got that box. But her husband Quiney broke it. It will not play its music any more. <u>Greensleeves and Pudding Pies</u> it used to play. And a tune called <u>Fortune's Maggot</u>. And <u>London Bridge Is Falling Down</u> as well.

Mr Shakespeare always thought of Hamnet and Judith together.

That was wrong of him.

That was a defect in love.

When Hamnet died, he thought Judith was just a ghost left.

He never liked it that she would not read.

He could not value it that she did nothing on purpose to please him.

My poor goose girl, with her shyness and her stubborn ways and her headaches and her clenched fists and now that sinner Quiney to put up with.

More followed.

And not trinkets.

I mean: it was not just at Christmas he remembered us.

Alas, that died the death in '92.

All that had stopped two years before the April of my story.

The plague hit London then.

The playhouses were shut down, them being pits of infection.

Mr Shakespeare wrote me a letter. So many were dying, he said, that the sextons would not even toll the bells for burials, because the tolling would have gone on night and day.

I thought he might come home then.

But he didn't.

Twenty-Nine
Hopping

To tell you the truth, that April afternoon I arrived in London, marching along with his Italian-cut peas porridge cloak about my shoulders, I hadn't much notion what my dear husband had been doing since the plague came.

I knew he had not died himself, that's all.

Certain small sums of money turned up regularly.

Enough to keep us going, just about.

But never a word to explain what was holding Mr Shakespeare there in London.

Why, for all I knew he might not have been in London. . . .

For all I knew then, Mr Shakespeare could have been spending his enforced holidays hopping to Norwich, say, in company with that joker Ned once told me of, Will Kemp.

Turning their backs on the plague, perhaps.

Fitted out with their own little bells.

Motley men, all men together.

Two clowns footing it merrily.

Two fools drinking all the way.

Just like in the bad days with his father.

Stopping at every whorehouse.

Counting ten miles as but a leap.
Two silly Morris-dancing madcaps!
More like St Vitus Dance, if you ask me –

Not so, neither.

    When it came down to it, either that April day or any other, I knew I could not possibly picture for long in my mind's eye the image of Mr Shakespeare hip-hopping from London to Norwich.

    Reader, he would not even walk the mile or so west to my father's farm at Shottery in the early days of our acquaintance.

    Not if he could beg or borrow a nag to ride on.

    Besides which, you must appreciate that I understand now how my husband's life was really in his writing.

    And it's hard to write on the hop, so I should say.

    Not that I knew yet, mind you, as I promenaded in that cloak along the dirty streets of London, that writing was now Mr Shakespeare's whole life.

    The husband beside me was almost a stranger to me.

Thirty
Egypt

Mr Shakespeare had lured me up to London with a letter.

It was a very curious letter.

I wish I still had it.

If I had, I would put it here in my book for you to read.

I remember the ending especially.

The ending was really peculiar.

It ended:

THINE EVERMORE, MOST DEAR LADY, WHILST
THIS MACHINE IS TO HIM, SHAKESPEARE.

I think you will agree that is a mighty peculiar way to end a letter.

When I read it, I wondered if Mr Shakespeare was going mad.

I think any honest wife or mother would agree with me.

However, the rest of that letter, while curious, was not so peculiar.

Are our bodies machines?

Well, I ask you.

Mad ending or not, I kept that strange letter for years in my treasure bag behind the bread-bin in the pantry.

Alas, one night a rat got in and ate it.

All gnawed and shredded, it wasn't worth keeping any more.

It was after that rat ate the letter that I got my cat for company.

She's a queen among cats.

I call her Egypt.

(Mr Shakespeare used to choose to annoy me by calling her Cleopatra. For short, he said. Although of course it is longer.)

My Egypt's too old for it now, but when she was in her prime she was forever having kittens.

Nothing and no one could stop her.

She had her litters in wardrobes and in cupboards, under the floorboards, on chairs, on the beds as well.

She had one not particularly messy litter on John and Susanna's bed. Dear John was furious. He would not sleep in the bed for three weeks, so great was his horror.

Men are queer creatures, when you get down to it.

They're like children sometimes.

Egypt is a beautiful cat, sleek-coated, bright-eyed, and remains a reliable mouser.

I'd rather have my necessary Egypt than that curious letter.

But I wish I still had the letter all the same.

Thirty-One
Mind-Reading

That letter of Mr Shakespeare's was full of grand vague talk of having something to celebrate as well as his thirtieth birthday.

So, all right, the plague had abated.

And I had heard already that the playhouses were soon to be opened again.

(Cousin Greene told me that. Red-headed Thomas Greene, my husband's kinsman, the lawyer in the Middle Temple who became Town Clerk of Stratford, now retired.)

And Mr Shakespeare had mentioned in his letter that Mr Burbage now required him to write a few plays of his own.

Comedies, he said.

Comedies and histories and tragedies.

But Mr Shakespeare had not said anything about payment in advance for these comedies and histories and tragedies.

And even if he had touched Mr Burbage for a little on account, I doubted if it would have been sufficient to inspire him to splash out for a suit like the one he was now strutting in.

Let alone that Italian-style cloak which was keeping me so elegant and warm.

Besides which, the garments were completely out of character.

I had never before seen Mr Shakespeare so popinjay-dressed.

My arm linked in his, I fingered the texture of his doublet and I wondered where he had got it.

How on earth could my out-of-work husband afford such dandy clothes?

Mr Shakespeare was always very good at guessing what I might be thinking.

It could be uncanny.

I got this pricking in my thumbs every time it happened.

One time, I remember, I was dreaming of a song and he began to sing it.

I thought at first that I must have been humming it, or drumming out the rhythm with my fingers, and he had heard me and given voice to the tune and the words.

But he had not heard anything, he assured me.

It was just that he knew me to be entertaining that melody in my head.

Another time I was busy counting sheep, trying to get to sleep, and he said, "Fifty-five!"

How in heaven's name he knew that I was counting sheep, let alone that I had just reached the fifty-fifth little bleater, I could not possibly explain for you.

There can be no natural explanations.

At such times he made me feel that the thin white bone in my forehead had become transparent.

At such times I considered him a warlock, almost.

*

Well, that day, the day of my story, as we were coming out of the shadow of the spire of some Romish-looking church, and treading our way into an offal pudding called (as I remember) Gracious Street, my husband glanced suddenly at me, sidelong, and said:

"That cloak. Someone gave me that cloak. I didn't buy it."

I elected to ignore the mind-reading.

It was too melancholy for present contemplation.

After all, here was further evidence that Mr Shakespeare sometimes knew what I was thinking, while I never had any idea what went on in his weird head.

It was too sad for words.

As for the cloak having been given to him: I was curious, of course, as to who was the giver. But I did not care to let Mr Shakespeare know of my interest.

So:

"I see," I said.

Mr Shakespeare smiled.

"I don't believe you do see," he remarked. "Let me explain. That summer's day comparison. I was joking."

"Oh, thanks again," I said. "Thanks very much."

"No, no," said Mr Shakespeare. "Don't be angry. The joke was at my own expense, I assure you. Shall I compare thee to a summer's day. . . . I was quoting myself. Something I wrote. A sonnet. The first line of it came back into my mind as we stood by London Bridge. I wrote this sonnet comparing someone to a summer's day. The person I wrote the sonnet about gave me the cloak."

I thought about all this news for a moment or two.

I began to wish that I was not wearing the cloak.

I wanted to be free of it, even if that meant being cold again.

I said nothing of these feelings.

Instead, I said:

"It must have been a good sonnet."

"Why?" asked Mr Shakespeare.

"Because it's a good cloak," I answered him.

My husband shrugged his shoulders.

"I suppose that sonnet wasn't bad," he said. "But I have done better."

¶ Thirty-Two
Blushes

I considered the peacock feather wagging in Mr Shakespeare's hat.

"Did you get your whole wardrobe from sonnets?" I asked him, quite pleasantly.

Mr Shakespeare blushed.

The blood rushed into his cheeks and remained there throbbing.

My husband was always a great blusher.

His face always answered to the emotions of the moment.

He was fair and he flushed easily. His colour was naturally high, and it got higher when the least thing made him bashful.

Were such blushes the emblem of his innocence, or his guilt?

Neither, I say.

I say the gentleman blushed because he had too much blood in him.

If he would have consented to be cupped, like Hamnet Sadler was when he had the sickness, then for sure the barber-surgeon could have cured it.

But Mr Shakespeare had a horror of blood-letting.

He preferred to suffer the agony of his own hot

blushes, though in the days when I first knew him he was not beyond seeking to remedy or soften the condition by such maid's tricks as cooling his face by washing it with nenuphar waters and lovage and the like.

And later in life Dr John Hall prescribed and supplied for him the water of frogs' spawn to apply to his burning cheeks, which was I believe some help.

But never quite did my husband lose this tendency to blush crimson when he was embarrassed.

You know what they say:

Blushing is some sign of grace.

All the same, I could find it astonishing.

I mean when you think what Mr Shakespeare did and what Mr Shakespeare said, and when you consider the kind of things Susanna says he wrote about, and how worldly and sophisticated a villain he was in so many other ways.

For such a man to go red in the face when his wife asked him the simple question if he had got his whole wardrobe from writing sonnets still seems to me nothing short of remarkable.

I have seen Mr Shakespeare do some very strange deeds in the grip of his bright blushes.

The blushing seemed to make him lose control.

Then he lashed out with some wild gesture to mask its happening.

Once when his mother was telling the story of his birth, and what a hard time she had had of it in having him, I watched him blush until his whole face must have hurt.

He sat nursing his cheeks in his hands while Mary went on and on with her account of the terrible labour.

Then up he jumped and popped a pickled onion in her mouth!

He made a joke of it, and his father laughed, but Mary nearly choked on that pickled onion.

Another time, when Mr Shakespeare was blushing, I observed him plunge head-first in a butt of malmsey, as if by that he might cool his cheeks again.

(But that was in the drunk days with his father.)

This time, in London, at that moment when I asked him if he had got his whole fashionable wardrobe from the writing of sonnets, and he began his big blush in response, Mr Shakespeare suddenly spun aside from me with one almighty kick.

For a second I thought he kicked for the sake of kicking.

Then I observed that his kick had a definite object.

The object of the kick was a passing cur.

It was a runt of a dog, as black as the backside of a chimney, with no tail, and a nose like a weasel's.

When Mr Shakespeare kicked it, it rose about six inches in the air, yelping, and then came splashing down in the mud of the street.

The black cur lay there, winded, its mouth wide open.

I noticed that it didn't have a tooth in its unfortunate head.

Its coat was mangy.

Then the black cur got up, and shook itself, and ran away barking.

My husband stood fingering his blush.

"You saw that?" he said. "It was going to bite you!"

I looked at him.

The blush gave his face the appearance of a rose.

"I saw that," I said. "I saw what you did."
The rose of Mr Shakespeare's face looked fit to burst.
"A savage dog," he said. "It was going to bite you!"
I should explain:
My husband was no dog-lover.

¶ Thirty-Three
Dogs

No, my Mr Shakespeare never did like dogs.

Cats he could tolerate, and my Egypt I think he admired.

Why, Egypt would sit upon his knee, and my husband was sometimes even known to stroke her fur.

That cat might lie curled about his naked foot too, on occasion, when he was writing, comforted by the way his toes tapped out the pattern of his poesy.

But dogs and Mr Shakespeare did not agree.

Fawning lapdogs, he called them, or else savage beasts.

Any dog with a master was the first kind, in his estimation. Any masterless mongrel might be the second.

Whoreson dogs, he called them all.

Our granddaughter Elizabeth had a lop-eared spaniel puppy when she was small.

Crab, we called it, because it liked to run sideways.

To amuse Elizabeth, for his little granddaughter's sake, Mr Shakespeare would throw sticks for Crab the puppy.

But he used to turn away and hurry indoors before the spaniel had the chance to bring them back, either to avoid commending or patting the dog for its effort, or to save himself the trouble of a second throw of the same stick.

That, though, was a major act of kindness in the record of my husband's doings with dogs.

Elizabeth's spaniel puppy Crab was the only dog I ever saw him even pretend to like.

¶ Thirty-Four
My Smile

All this considered, the blush and the dog-hating, I cannot say that I was surprised when Mr Shakespeare kicked that cur in Gracious Street.

The dog's savagery I preferred not to comment upon, to my husband.

To you, dear Reader, I might observe that if that dog had bitten me, it would have hurt its toothless gums.

"Well, did you?" I asked Mr Shakespeare again.

"Did I what?" said he.

"Did you derive your whole wardrobe from writing sonnets?" said I.

The blush spread.

It travelled down Mr Shakespeare's throat to his Adam's apple.

It journeyed right across to his ears.

He had big ears.

The blush entered them.

His ears raged with it.

The blush had become a great rash now.

The sly eyes of Mr Shakespeare went this way and that way in the street.

He looked anywhere and everywhere, at anything

and at nothing, just to save himself from meeting my frank gaze.

He was gnawing at his fingernails.

"More or less," he admitted. "I suppose I did."

Mr Shakespeare spat.

His nails must have tasted bitter to him, I reckon.

Mr Shakespeare said:

"But I didn't write the sonnets to get the clothes."

"Of course not," I said. "Of course you didn't."

Mr Shakespeare said:

"I just got the clothes for the sonnets."

"Of course, of course," I said. "Of course you did."

Mr Shakespeare seized both his blushing ear-lobes in his fingers, and tweaked and tugged at them, at the same time crying:

"And I only wrote the sonnets because I *had* to!"

I favoured him with a smile I had been *practising*.

"I understand you perfectly," I said.

I should perhaps explain my practised smile.

I had been told that I lacked sympathy.

(I do not think I do. It was said I did.)

Judith Sadler said so. My friend Judith said that when she told me about her husband Hamnet's snoring the look on my face had not been sympathetic.

Now, since I knew very well that in fact I *did* sympathise, I could only conclude that my face had not been a true index to my feelings on this occasion.

I knew that I had smiled at Judith (as I hoped, with sympathy), but perhaps my smile had not expressed what I was feeling.

For this reason I had been studying before my glass.

I would stare at myself in my looking-glass and smile from the heart by the minute.

It did cross my mind that there was a something false in this action, something a touch actorish or whorish, something lacking in integrity.

And the result could turn patronising if held there too long on my lips.

All the same, I wanted the shape of my smile to match what I knew my smiling meant.

Meaning is all, and the face is where we show what we mean to each other.

Therefore, I had been learning how to smile well.

My eyes of course played a very big part in this.

The lips may lie, but the eyes always tell you the truth.

I'm talking about reality, not art.

I'm talking about true semblance, not dissembling.

I did not have bad teeth that I wanted to hide.

Sir Smile himself did not deserve this smile of mine.

His blushing, his kicking of the cur, his stammering defence and self-justification of his sonnet-mongering, these things did not add up to a need for my smile.

Yet kindness will creep where it cannot walk upright in company.

So I smiled for Mr Shakespeare.

I smiled at him.

It was then that it started to rain, as I remember.

Small rain began falling from a sky that was the colour of duck's eggs.

Mr Shakespeare bit his lower lip.

I waited, smiling.

He took me by the arm, and we walked on.

¶ Thirty-Five
My Sonnet

This is a very sad story that I am telling you.

It's a love story of sorts, as I hope you may have realised by now.

I think the saddest stories are always our stories about love.

Mr Shakespeare wrote sonnets when I first knew him.

He wrote a sonnet for me once when he had annoyed me in some trifle and I (for I was quick-tempered in those days) made a sound from which he supposed that I must hate him.

It happened like this.

He was forever presenting himself as lovelorn and ill-used in those early days of our acquaintance.

One time I turned away from him impatiently, when he was being importunate in his demands, and he annoyed me very much by pretending that if I was not kind to him his heart would stop!

Well, what would you have done?

I could not help it.

I made some disgusted mocking sound.

I think any honest woman would have done the same.

But young Mr Shakespeare took my displeasure with his behaviour as expressing my hatred for him.

And when I saw how deep downcast he was then, with tears starting to his eyes, I had pity on him.

I clucked my tongue as though I was chiding it for the very disapproving noise that I had made, and I said, "Not you!"

Whereupon he said, "What do you mean? You hate me!"

And I said: "I hate it when you pretend so. But I do not hate you."

Which of course I know now that I am older and wiser to be perfectly sound religion.

For we should hate the sin, yet love the sinner.

At all events, Mr Shakespeare waxed mighty pleased and then thoughtful when I said this I hate it when you pretend so, but I do not hate you.

He walked up and down muttering it to himself for half an hour or more.

He quite forgot in this new passion the kisses and such that he'd been after in the first place.

And the next time he came calling at Hewlands Farm he handed me this sonnet which he had made upon the matter:

THOSE LIPS THAT LOVE'S OWN HAND DID MAKE
BREATH'D FORTH THE SOUND THAT SAID "I
    HATE",
TO ME THAT LANGUISH'D FOR HER SAKE:
BUT WHEN SHE SAW MY WOEFUL STATE,
STRAIGHT IN HER HEART DID MERCY COME,
CHIDING THAT TONGUE THAT EVER SWEET
WAS USED IN GIVING GENTLE DOOM;

AND TAUGHT IT THUS ANEW TO GREET;
"I HATE" SHE ALTER'D WITH AN END,
THAT FOLLOW'D IT AS GENTLE DAY
DOTH FOLLOW NIGHT, WHO, LIKE A FIEND,
FROM HEAVEN TO HELL IS FLOWN AWAY;
"I HATE" FROM HATE AWAY SHE THREW,
AND SAV'D MY LIFE, SAYING "NOT YOU."

Permit me to make this plain for any reader who is not accustomed to the kind of riddling speech you find in poesy.

In line one, he means that I have a good mouth.

In line seven, when he says my tongue was used in giving gentle doom he means that my tongue usually gave him gentle judgements.

In line thirteen, when he says "I hate" from hate away she threw he means that I took away the meaning of hatred from the noise of disgust and disapproval I had not been able to contain, by saying (line fourteen) "not you."

All this is very intricate and witty, and of course it is also quite ridiculous to say as he does (lines ten and eleven) that my adding the "not you" was like changing night to day, especially when the harmless necessary night is then compared (lines eleven and twelve) to a fiend who has to fly away from heaven to hell.

All that kind of big talk is only too common in poesy, I'm afraid.

I make no apology for it.

I, too, dislike it.

The line, by the way, which Mr Shakespeare was especially pleased with himself for writing was the thirteenth:

"I hate" from hate away she threw. . . .

When I first read the sonnet, I made no comment
on this particular line, which annoyed him hugely.

Whereupon he read the whole thing aloud,
stressing the *"I hate" from hate away* bit.

I fear that I still failed to get the point.

Then Mr Shakespeare cried:

"Hate away! Hathaway! Don't you see? A play on
your name, Anne!"

I suppose that it is clever.

As clever as a monkey's tricks.

But then I don't like monkeys.

Mr Shakespeare also boasted:

"One day someone will read it and know it was
you! That I hid your name there! The name of my love
who said and did these things to me!"

I suppose he might be right.

But then that's another trouble with poesy.

When poets are not caressing themselves with their
own words, they're busy a-courting posterity.

They spend a lot of the time admiring the
lineaments of their own minds. Then off they go on the
look-out for future admirers, putting things in just to
impress them or so that such readers can flatter themselves
by their discovery.

Poets use their poems like looking-glasses in the
first place, and then in the second place as caskets where
they can conceal the precious jewels of their own
wit.

Am I right?

I am.

Well, it makes me sick.

Anyway, this hate away/Hathaway nonsense will suffice at least to let you see that Mr Shakespeare was an old hand and a dab one when it came to the sonnets trade.

As we tripped along through the rain I could not help wondering, of course, what it might be that had caused him to start off writing them again these days in London.

He had come up with sonnets like neat fourteen-line rhyming answers to problems in our early life together.

It was as though he thought he could resolve any falling out by putting it all down pat in a sonnet with a couplet at the end to bring us together once more.

Which was all very well at the time, and did no lasting harm, but still left me with the question:

Who was Mr Shakespeare trying to solve problems with now?

Reader, I was curious.

Reader, I was interested.

Reader, I was worried.

However, I was also getting wet, so I said nothing.

Thirty-Six
Cherries

Mr Shakespeare was getting wet too, but he didn't seem
to mind.

In fact, my getting wet husband looked relieved.

He looked as if he was glad that he had got the
confession of sonneting off his chest.

He looked as if he had unpacked his bowels of some
worm that was poisoning him.

The blush faded.

It ebbed from his cheeks.

Soon he was his old familiar self again. Soon he
had his old familiar face back.

I examined that face, sidelong, as we walked.

Here is what I saw:

Mr Shakespeare's face was frank, though there was always
something sly going on in his eyes.

His features were firm, yet delicate.

His eyebrows were fair, and set low.

His forehead was bald.

He had a slight downy moustache, and a small lip
beard above his strong smooth chin.

There was a mole on his left cheek.

His most singular feature was without doubt his nose — which was broader at the nostrils than it was down the straight, solid bridge.

It was oval in shape, that face, with hazel eyes that roved to and fro with an errant foxy look for much of the time, but which stared through you when they came to rest upon you.

It was the face of a man who looked as if he could have got drunk on moonlight.

It was the face of his father's son.

The rain trickled down Mr Shakespeare's face as we hurried along through the shower.

I noticed his tongue flicking out now and then in quest of a taste of the raindrops.

As I say, he looked purged by what he had told me, as by the gentle rain.

We hastened on without speaking for a while.

Then Mr Shakespeare stopped a pedlar woman.

He produced a fat purse from his doublet and he bought me a handful of red cherries.

I was not ungrateful.

I appreciated not so much the cherries but the thoughtfulness which made my husband suppose that I might stand in need of a bite to eat.

All the same, cherries. . . .

I wanted more than cherries, I can tell you.

I could have done with a rabbit stew, or a nice mutton pie piping-hot!

I remember the raindrops silvering my peas porridge cloak, and that red-cheeked pedlar woman.

She looked as though she had been infected by my husband's previous blush.

I remember the rain falling between the steeples

out of that lowering London sky, and that red-cheeked woman standing in the rain in her black shawl and handing me the cherries in a little poke of paper.

I ate one of those cherries.

It tasted of London and the woman.

I did not like the way that cherry tasted.

I did not care for the things that cherry tasted of.

I determined to have it out with Mr Shakespeare.

"Sonnets," I said.

"Yes," he said. "Sonnets."

"So have you written many?" I demanded.

My husband frowned.

I could see that he despised me for what he considered my weakness in wanting to count them.

However, it was not just for the sake of a passion for arithmetic that I wanted to know.

Mr Shakespeare sighed.

"I must have written more than a hundred now," he said, without enthusiasm.

"Fancy," said I.

"Yes," Mr Shakespeare said. "A century plus of sonnets."

"Well, well," I said.

I didn't eat any more cherries.

I did not feel like eating cherries any more.

I was, of course, still hungry.

I could still have done with something good and hot.

I could have fancied even a piece of powdered beef as green as a leek.

As for pork sausages, I could have murdered some.

But I just couldn't face those cherries any more.

Thirty-Seven
Ant and Glove

*Funny how you can go right off a particular item of your
food, isn't it?*

I remember once I was eating some lovely little pears.

*They were yellow pears, round, and hard, and good,
and their peel was so thin, and their pips were black as
jet.*

*First I pulled out the tiny straight stem from the
top of each pear and I sucked it.*

*That stem tasted sour, but the pears were as sweet
as could be.*

I ate each pear from the top, quickly, core and all.

*I must have eaten six of them like this, a half a
dozen sweet little yellow pears, plump and good, but then
just as I was about to eat the last one in the basket I saw
that an ant had got into it.*

*I can still see that tiny round hole with a sort of
fringe of brown pepper round it where the ant had got in.*

After that, I could not eat the final pear.

In fact I never ate those little yellow pears again.

This was not revulsion.

*It was the idea that any such pear might be the
home of an ant.*

*

I remember another time I'd made this excellent fish-bake.

I spent all night dreaming of it, all morning making it, all afternoon baking it.

But, before supper, something went wrong.

It was only a small thing, but it put me right off my meal.

What happened first was that a fly got into the kitchen and buzzed about, and then in the pocket of an old coat hanging on a nail on the back door I found one of Mr Shakespeare's gloves – a fine cheveril glove with two black buttons to do up at the wrist.

It must have been there for years in the pocket.

I held that cheveril glove against my cheek and I could smell my husband.

Then I swatted the fly with it.

After that, I could not face my own pie.

I don't know why, but I just could not face my own splendid fish-bake.

I'd been so looking forward to eating that pie. But then, after finding the cheveril glove and using it to swat the fly that had come into the kitchen, I discovered I'd completely lost my appetite.

Remove far from me vanity and lies: give me neither poverty nor riches; feed me with food convenient for me (Proverbs, 30, viii).

Mr Shakespeare was born with poor unhappy brains for drinking.

He lay between two silver candlesticks.

I put my arms about his neck.

He smiled.

"Hang there like fruit," he said. "Hang there like fruit, my soul, till the tree die."

He must have thought that he was standing up.
Then all his face went blind.

I'm wandering again.
Well, it's only human nature, isn't it?

¶ Thirty-Eight
Not a She

Then it stopped raining, I remember that.

The April shower ceased.

It stopped its raining at about the moment I found no stomach in myself for those London cherries.

A noise of musicians went down the street past us.

There were two flutes, four fiddles, a rebeck, a shawm, and a treble viol, also a boy with a bumbard.

They followed their leader as diligent as little chickens after a hen.

I clapped my hands, and listened. But my husband appeared anxious to be gone.

That puzzled me. He enjoyed music, usually.

When the band had marched away around the corner we resumed our own slow progress.

But straight away as we did, I smiled at him, saying:

"I'm glad, you know."

"What about?" asked Mr Shakespeare.

"I'm glad you told me about your writing of your sonnets."

"I see," said Mr Shakespeare.

"It's very good to know," I told him, sweetly.

My husband frowned.

"What's good to know? That I've written so many sonnets?"

"No," I said. "What's good to know is that you have someone to write so many sonnets *for*."

Mr Shakespeare hung his head.

The feather in his hat cast a shadow down his face. It had got bedraggled. The rain had not done that peacock's feather any favours at all. That feather looked more like an emblem of pride's failure by the minute.

I spelt out my displeasure for my scowling husband, keeping my voice childish and sentimental as I did so.

"What's good to know is that you have someone," I said. "What's good to know is that you have someone to write your sonnets for. What's very good to know is that this someone you have to write your sonnets for is the sort of someone you have to write so *many* sonnets for."

I seized his arm and stopped him in his stride.

I held out my hand to his face.

His mouth fell open.

I popped a fat cherry into it.

"And to get *paid* in kind," I said.

Mr Shakespeare was choking.

"More than a hundred," I said. "She must dote on sonnets."

I smacked Mr Shakespeare on the back.

He swallowed the cherry, stone and all.

"She must be a real adäict," I said. "She must be some sort of sonnet-freak."

My husband was coughing and spluttering.

He was waving his hands in the air.

He was going bright red in the face again.

"What's that?" I cried. "What's that you're trying to say?"

I half-thought it might be an apology.

Let me tell you, I hoped for an apology.
More fool me.
What I got was no apology, God knows.
Mr Shakespeare took a deep breath and then
cleared his throat.
"It isn't a she," Mr Shakespeare said.

My husband.
Queer Mr Shakespeare.
Love's apostate.

Thirty-Nine
Hemlock

I tripped on the hem of that peas porridge cloak.

   I trod in a heap of horse-manure.

   At least, I think that what I trod in then was horse-manure.

   It could have been man-manure for all I know.

   It might have been his father's, if his father had been visiting London.

   It might have been Mr Shakespeare's for that matter.

   (We were not very far from his lodgings now.)

   There it was in Gracious Street: a little golden dungheap.

   I trod in it.

   I tripped and trod in the stuff.

Here are some other ways to spell my husband's name:

   Shagsper.

   Shaxpure.

   Shakeshafte.

   Chacsper.

   Spell it any way that takes your fancy.

   Spell it any way you like or which you don't like.

I make no bones about it, Reader:
I was displeased.

Because, O yes, I knew what my husband meant.
Just because I had passed most of my days in the
town of Stratford doesn't mean I had not heard of
Platonism.
I knew that unspeakable things went on between
Socrates and his disciples.
I knew they made that Greek take hemlock for it.
And look what happened to those young men in the
city of Sodom when they went too far in entertaining
angels.

He that loves not womankind, cannot be counted
mankind.
Well, I ask you.

Forty
A New Beginning

I began this book of mine with words of his.

That was wrong, I see now.

Am I to be his shadow?

I am not.

So should I be his echo?

No, I say.

I should have begun my book with words of my own.

Go back, therefore, and undo my first sentence, will you?

Wipe out all memory of it from your mind.

Let Mrs Shakespeare's book begin:

"NO THANKS!"

Forty-One
Footnote

Oh yes, and that peas porridge cloak was long on me.
Remember?

I'm the ten and three quarter inches shorter than
Mr Shakespeare was.

What was a calf-length job on him was a
full-length job on me.

That's how (in case you were wondering) it came
to pass that I should trip on the hem of the cloak.

Go tripping and then treading in manure.

This, if you will pardon me the pun, is a footnote
to the first sentence of my hemlock chapter. (Number 39).

I despise all writers who stoop as low as puns.

I give you my word no more will disfigure these
pages.

Forty-Two
Rizley

"So," said I to Mr Shakespeare, "did it rain?"

"What?" he said.

"That summer's day sonnet," I said. "Was there rain in it?"

Mr Shakespeare frowned.

I watched him running through his sonnet in his head, trying very hard to remember the weather.

"I don't think so," he said, at last. "No. No rain."

"I see," I said.

He stared at me, baffled.

"What the devil," said he, "has rain got to do with it?"

"I just wondered," I said. "I just wondered if your sonnets were being written to advertise cloaks. It crossed my mind that your inspirer might perhaps be a cloak-maker."

My husband let go of my arm then.

He blew on his hand as if what I'd just said had stung it.

"As a matter of fact," he said, "the man we are talking about is of noble birth."

This did not surprise me.

I've told you of his liking for the lordly ones.

Mr Shakespeare was always a snob.

"I see," I said. "Is he rich?"

Mr Shakespeare shrugged.

At least, I think he shrugged.

I've said a couple of times in this narrative that my husband shrugged, but truth to tell I should have said only that I do believe he shrugged.

As I've told you, he was wearing a fancy doublet.

Now I noticed that the shoulders of this doublet were so puffed that what I took then for a shrug might have been only a twitch of embarrassment.

I like to be accurate.

A shrug would imply indifference to the richness of the friend. Or, at the least, an affectation of such indifference displayed for my benefit.

Whereas a twitch would mean, rather, embarrassment.

Or irritation, that I dare ask such a question.

And what Mr Shakespeare's shoulders were expressing could just as well have been that.

I linked my arm in his again.

I was hurt and puzzled, but I wanted to comprehend.

I determined to look upon the bright side.

I look upon the bright side when I can.

"Don't fret," I said. "I'm pleased for you."

"Are you?" Mr Shakespeare said, doubtfully.

"I am," I said.

"Really and truly?" Mr Shakespeare said.

"Really and truly," I said. "There's no money in poesy, is there? Any poet's wife knows that. Poets need patrons. You've been lucky to find one."

"Henry's more than a patron," Mr Shakespeare said. "Henry's my friend."

"Henry?" I said. "So that's his name? Henry?"

"Henry Rizley," Mr Shakespeare said.

We paused to let a cart turn into a brewer's yard without killing us.

I took the chance to drop the rest of the cherries down a drain.

Then we walked on up past the Cornhill, arm in arm.

"Henry Rizley," my husband said, "Earl of Southampton."

"Hang on," I said.

"What's the matter?" said Mr Shakespeare.

"I want to scrape this horse-shit off my boot-soles," I told him.

Mr Shakespeare watched me while I did it.

"And Baron of Tichfield," he said, rubbing his long nose.

My neat's-skin boots cleaned, we resumed our way into Bishopsgate.

"Earl of Southampton," I recited, "and Baron of Tichfield. Some patron!"

"I told you, Anne," said my husband, "Henry's not just a patron –"

"I haven't forgotten," I told him. "He's more like a summer's day, isn't he?"

Once, when I was a child, I stood beneath a cherry tree in blossom on Stinchcombe Hill.

It was early in the morning.

I raised my hand. I beckoned with my forefinger.

A single petal fell into my hand.
That was the beginning.

John always says it was an apoplexy.
Mr Shakespeare's head being full of
hammerdryads.
This made his left temporal artery very thick, John
says.
John treated him with a poultice made of a
swallow's nest, dirt, dung, and all, boiled in oil of
chamomel and lilies, beaten and passed through a sieve,
to which was added white dog's turd one ounce.
I say it was sack and canary killed him, it was
malmsey and muscadel.
I blame that Drayton and that Jonson. (And,
before them, that Quiney didn't help.)
Those poets didn't stay for the funeral, even.
The sheet was frayed where he gnawed it with his
teeth.
I washed his dirty linen.
I put pennies on his eyes.
I was his mother and his wife who has now to be
his widow.

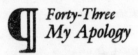

Forty-Three
My Apology

Here we are, Reader!

We have reached Mr William Shakespeare's lodgings!

And I do apologise that it has taken us so long to get here.

I mean, in one way this must have been about the slowest walk in words you ever had.

It has taken me 122 pages of my little vellum-bound book to get me and Mr Shakespeare from London Bridge to the door of his London lodgings.

I'm sorry.

I am not a good writer.

I'm afraid I am not a real writer at all.

Mr Shakespeare would have got us here in a trice.

He'd have shaken his warlock's wand of words and we'd have been here.

I have no magic wand. I have only the goose-quill of truth.

That's the difference between me and Mr Shakespeare, as between truth and poesy.

I cannot cut corners.

I have to tell it to you as it was.

I spell it all out. I explain. I explicate. I do not

make grand word-noises for your pleasure.

Still and all, though, 122 pages for a walk across London!

I tried to speed things up in that last chapter.

It goes against the grain, but I did try.

I hope you noticed?

All those <u>he saids</u> and <u>I saids</u>.

That's how real writers do it.

But doing that means leavings out, you know.

For instance, when we got to the bit about his Rizley friend being the Earl of Southampton and the Baron of Tichfield and I reminded you of my husband's liking for the lordly ones, it was in my mind to mention that Sir Thomas Lucy business back here in Stratford.

But then, perhaps, the least said about such a fiasco the soonest mended.

To steal a man's deer because he won't help you get on!

I choose, therefore, to leave that out, for my husband's best sake. I am not in the humour to gratify curiosity in this matter.

Nor shall I bother to repeat his lousy Lucy libel. It was, in fact, a dead bore.

Talking of libels, though, I haven't forgotten John Lane.

You see, there are stories I'm having to tell you along with our story.

This is the story of the poet, the wife, the best bed, and the bed called second-best.

But it is also in some part the story of John Shakespeare who began as an ale-taster for the Stratford council and ended as a drunkard, and of Mary Arden his wife (that saint), and of Susanna my swan and Judith my goose, and of Dr John Hall my learned good son-in-law, and of my other son-in-law Thomas Quiney (that sinner) of The Cage.

If you tell a true story truly then you find other stories to tell.

I tell you the one story, but I tell other stories as well.

Forty-Four
Warning

But here we are at last at the door of Mr Shakespeare's London lodgings.

In Bishopsgate, by St Helen's, as he said.

We have walked together through the streets of little hell.

And we stand on the threshold, now, of my tale proper.

When once we go in through this door there is no turning back.

We go in through this door together, me and Mr Shakespeare, and you, Reader, will have to go in through this door with us.

You must climb the stairs with us.

You will have to be a part of what we find there.

Reader, I falter.

I stop at this juncture to warn you:

Turn away now if you have not the heart and the stomach of the lion.

Courage, my Reader!

You shall receive reward of the truth revealed.

Love's secret truth is always worth knowing, I say.

And I say that we are the stronger, the better, and

the wiser, for knowing each other's love-weaknesses and follies and errors in love.

Yet the truth I have soon to reveal to you is strong meat indeed, and you should be warned.

Forty-Five
Hare Soup

For that reason, why not try some good hare soup?

I always say a bowl of good hare soup works wonders.

Besides, it's a wonder to me that writers never think to offer their readers any advice as to what they might be eating while they read.

What greater pleasure than to read and to eat at the same time?

So long as one is not required to be in company, reading while eating strikes me as a civilised joy.

And since tonight I have made myself a bowl of good hare soup, and since I would like to think of you as sharing it, here, Reader, is my recipe for:

MRS SHAKESPEARE'S EXCELLENT
HARE SOUP

Take a hare. Skin it, taking care not to break the inside.

Put in your hand and take out the lungs.

Hold your hare over a basin and catch his blood.

Cut up your hare into pieces.

Take all his bones out, and lay the fleshy parts aside.

Now put all the bones into a pot, cover well with water (cold), and add turnip, carrot, stalk of celery, and a few onions.

Boil (if your hare is young) for 1½ hours.

Boil (if an old hare) for 2 hours or longer.

Pour your hare's blood through a hair sieve, then add some water, put in a handful of fine oatmeal and put into a stewpan.

Stir it one way till it boils.

But be careful not to let it curdle.

Take out bones.

Bruise vegetables well through a sieve.

Add the blood which has already been boiled.

Cut the flesh into small pieces (about the size of groats) and put in with the rest into the pot.

Boil all together, stirring well, for 1½ hours (longer by half an hour for your older hare).

Season with bistort.

Pepper and salt to taste.

Plus a small spoon of honey if you're like my Mr Shakespeare was.

Reader, I like to think of you taking some time away from my story to make your hare soup.

Be sure, that soup will fortify you for what is to come.

Why, you need that hare soup, Reader, if you are determined to go in now through this door with me and Mr Shakespeare.

How I wish that someone had provided me with a bowl of hot hare soup before I went in to my doom!

PART THREE
What Mr Shakespeare
Did To Me
The Only Time
I Ever Went to London

Forty-Six
Whelks

My husband's lodgings were over this wet fishmonger's on the corner of Turnagain Lane.

Outside was all fish-heads and fish-tails and tubs of live eels.

The inside seemed decent enough, but it did smell of mackerel.

I like fish, myself.

I like plaice and whiting.

I delight in broiled red sprat.

A nice brown trout well-baked in breadcrumbs would be my idea of a feast.

I can even enjoy conger, crab, and lamprey, so long as they come doused in oatmeal pap.

Whelks would be the only fish that I can't stomach.

And then I like them but they don't like me.

Forty-Seven
The Blindfold

At the foot of the back stairs of his lodgings in Turnagain Lane, Mr Shakespeare stopped and kissed me.

This was the first time he had kissed me since a peck on my cheek as I stepped from the carrier's cart on my arrival in London that afternoon.

His kiss was soft and watery.

It tasted of herring.

No master of osculation, William Shakespeare.

Am I right?

I am.

I should know, shouldn't I?

My husband twitched his nostrils and he kissed me.

And then he started unwinding this silk sash from the sleeve of his dandy doublet.

"What's the game then?" I asked Mr Shakespeare.

"A blindfold," said he. "I'd like you to wear it. I know what's up those stairs and you do not. I want to make it more of a surprise, that's all."

"Couldn't I just shut my eyes?" I asked him.

"It wouldn't be the same," Mr Shakespeare said.

"Why not?" I demanded. "I'd play fair. I promise not to open my eyes and look until you say so."

My husband sighed, and shook his enormous head.

"You know I hate surprises," I reminded him.

"You won't hate this one," Mr Shakespeare said.

It's true that I hate surprises, whether they're good or they're bad.

At birthdays and Christmasses, I am always a terrible feeler of packages.

I like to work out what is in there, concealed by the wrappings.

That way I know what expression to have on my face when the gift is opened up.

I detest it when anyone comes up and surprises me as well.

People touching you suddenly, without word or warning – that gives me the creeps.

And if I am scouring the pots and someone comes up behind me at the sink and tickles me, or gives me a prod in the ribs, that makes me jump out of my skin, I don't mind telling you, and I do not like it at all.

Mr Shakespeare stood there holding the silk sash out.

"Do I have to be blindfold?" I said.

He answered me very sly, very soft, like a mouse in cheese:

"Oh, you do! You do, my dear, yes!"

My husband was never what I would call a handsome man, but now his face was all at once boyish and eager.

And, against my better judgement, I was intrigued.

I admit it:

I felt this shiver of excitement run down my spine.

The blindfold bit was teasing.

It suggested some strange treat, some childish game.

Yet he was not a child, and nor was I, and somehow I knew that it could be nothing childish that awaited me.

Was it because I was being asked to behave so small in approaching something unknown that I felt the shiver?

Maybe so.

Something like that.

Something to do with a mystery.

Something to do with a treat.

And I hadn't had so many treats from Mr Shakespeare, not since the maypole days so long ago.

Forty-Eight
Up the Stairs

So I humoured my wag of a husband.

I gave in to his whim.

(Though I think, looking back now, that he planned every move he made.)

Whim or plan, I let him bind my eyes up with his blindfold.

I let him tie that sash around my head.

It felt smooth and warm. It was warm from his fingers where he had been twisting it this way and that as he sought to persuade me.

Then Mr Shakespeare took me by the hand.

He led me upstairs.

His hand was hot and sticky.

It was shaking.

His hand was shaking so much I thought he must have the fever.

And he had.

But not the kind of fever doctors cure.

We said nothing as we climbed.

He held my elbow.

The stairs were narrow. We were pressed quite close together as we went up them.

I felt the heat in Mr Shakespeare from the touch

of his body. Not just the heat of his hand. The heat of the whole man.

If you have never done it, I must tell you that it is strange being blindfold and going upstairs with a man guiding you by the elbow.

I felt completely at Mr Shakespeare's mercy.

Those stairs were steep.

They creaked as we climbed up them.

Otherwise the place was silent as the tomb.

But it was of course a tomb that stank of fishes.

We climbed right on up to the top.

I heard the sound of Mr Shakespeare unlocking a door, and the rasp of unoiled hinges as it opened.

He took my arm again and we went in.

I heard the closing and the locking of the door behind us.

"Just a minute," whispered Mr Shakespeare.

I heard the rattle of a tinderbox.

I smelt brimstone matches.

Then he took the blindfold off me, and I saw it.

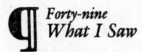

Forty-nine
What I Saw

That bed.

     "Jesu!" I cried. "It's like some Papist altar!"

¶ Fifty
The Bed

It was a gigantic four-poster, each post as thick as a man, with heavy crimson velvet curtains hanging right down to the floor from the canopy, and fat gold cords that dangled like bell-ropes.

It was the biggest four-poster bed that I ever saw.

When you pulled the curtains back you could see that the bed itself was decked out with a silk coverlet, black as night, all crusted with embroidery of stars.

It had half a dozen white pillows, stuffed with swansdown by the fat soft look of them, and lots of bolsters, and mattresses piled so high you needed a small step-ladder to get to the top.

As for its sheets, they were huge and begilt and gorgeous as sails ripped off some Spanish galleon of the Great Armada.

There were these seven black candles in silver sockets all along the bed's headboard, and the headboard itself was carved over with nymphs and things like goats.

Only they weren't goats.

I saw that at once as Mr Shakespeare crouched lighting the black candles.

It was not goats at that bed's head.

It was more devils.

Fifty-One
A Playhouse

So there was I crying "Jesu! It's like some Papist altar!"
as I stared at that monstrous great bed which seemed to fill
most of the gloomy shuttered room above the wet
fishmonger's in Turnagain Lane, and there was my
husband Mr William Shakespeare standing leaning
against one of the bed-posts and grinning at me.

He had lit all the candles along the carved
headboard.

His eyes were as bright as beads in the flickering
candlelight.

His face was pale, with these tiny seeds of sweat
trickling down it.

I watched that sweat splash.

It splashed on his shoes, drop, drip, drop.

Mr Shakespeare's shoes were black, with bright new
silver buckles.

His face seemed to shine in the candlelight.

Not just with sweat.

His face was shining as I stared at him.

Candlelight flattered Mr Shakespeare, but his head looked
as usual two sizes too big for his body.

His lips were dry and cracked.

His tongue was flicking in and out between them like a viper's.

He still held the sash in his left hand.

He mopped his face with it.

He sniffed it before and after he mopped his face with it.

Did he smell my scent off that sash?

Or was it his own sweat that he wanted to smell?

"Not an altar," Mr Shakespeare said. "A playhouse."

He started stroking his bony nose with the door-key.

Then he was tickling his little moustache with that key.

Fifty-Two
Play

"I have brought the playhouse here for you," Mr
Shakespeare said.

He pointed to the bed with the silver key.

I frowned at him, puzzled.

"I wouldn't know if it looks like a playhouse or not,"
I said. "I've never been in a playhouse in my life."

Mr Shakespeare kept grinning.

"Then isn't it time that you started?" said he.

I did not understand him.

I needed something to do, to conceal my confusion.

So I took off the peas porridge cloak.

I stood trembling in the gloom of that candlelit
room.

I was feeling apprehensive.

I had no wish to visit the playhouses, thank you.

Dens of vice.

Pits of illusion.

Places of make-believe.

Life is too short for going to the playhouse.

"This bed," Mr Shakespeare said. "This is our
private playhouse."

"Oh yes?" I said. "And what do we do in it?"
"We play," Mr Shakespeare said, smiling.

My husband.
Playful Mr Shakespeare.
The bottled spider.

Fifty-Three
The Point of My Story

Now you might think I don't need to tell you what Mr Shakespeare had in mind.

You might suppose, Reader, that I don't have to tell you what happened in that bed that night.

And the next day, his birthday.

And the next night.

And all the nights and the days of the week that followed.

But I do, because it wasn't exactly the usual.

And it not being exactly the usual is the point of my story.

Fifty-Four
The Lambskin Jacket

I had brought Mr Shakespeare a gift up from Stratford for his birthday.

Now I chose to unwrap it.

It was a jacket of black and white lambskins to keep out the cold.

Not a seasonable present perhaps, nor at all fashionable.

Yet there was a certain wifely loving-kindness in my choice, since I did not anticipate him being at home with me the following winter, or for any other winter for some time to come.

It was a handsome jacket.

Well-stitched.

Lined with sarcanet.

I held it up for my husband's inspection.

"Did you make this with your own hands?" he enquired.

"I did," I lied. "Happy birthday."

Mr Shakespeare kissed me then.

Then he took the jacket and kissed it.

He knew such tasks were not to my taste at all.

He knew that his wife was no seamstress.

"Try it on," I suggested.

He did.

He put on that lambskin jacket.

Then he stood there, still grinning foolishly, beside the enormous bed.

That grin was a mistake.

I could see those two broken black teeth.

He was twisting strands of his thin hair forwards to hide the baldness at his temples.

"I'm a wolf now," Mr Shakespeare said. "A wolf in sheep's clothing."

Then he took off my gown and my linen smock and my stockings, and he laid me down on that bed and we made love.

Fifty-Five
Love-making

The love that we made was not good.

This didn't surprise me, I must say.

Right from the start, even that first time at Welford by the millpool, it was always the imagined, the longed-for relish that enchanted Mr Shakespeare's senses.

My husband's palate when it came to the main course was what you might call watery.

He shrank from the act. He had no tongue for the nectar.

A sugarplate creature himself, he lacked thirst and bite.

All the same, my marchpane man got me pregnant with Susanna by that pool.

I was the three months gone when we were married.

"O my love," he said. "O my life."
"O my life," I said. "O my love."

Love?

No, it was not really love that we were making.
He could not.

And I would not.
And that's all.

*My husband had always been less than a man should be
in the labours of love.*
I tell you the plain truth now.
The unhappy fact of the matter.
*As God is my witness, our marriage bed never had
been good.*
No bliss, no place of sudden paradise or ease.
Not what it should have been.
*Why, even that first time, in the long grass, under
the catkins, when first he tickled trout then tickled me,
when you would think that perhaps the novelty might have
inspired him. . . .*
Well, it didn't.
I make no bones about it.
I'm sure the trout had a better time than I did.

Let me die if I lie.
*He proved no ardent wooer that afternoon at
Welford.*
*No great shakes, Mr Shakespeare, when it came to
it.*
Ha! (and Alas!)
His very name a joke.
Mine too, mind you.
*Because, you may be sure, Reader, I had my way
with him and of him.*
*I mean: It was me that did the hard work, or most
of it, to untie my own unwelcome virgin knot.*
(I gave him that greatest gift a girl can give.)
*O he was excited all right. He was quite giddy with
expectation.*

But then, as I learned soon enough, there was always this impediment in him which came between desire and its performance.

How can I put it?

Mr Shakespeare was a sweet lecher but he was not a lusty man.

He lusted after sweetness, but he lacked muscle.

His function in my department was not sufficient.

And now, that night on that bed, that night before he reached his thirtieth birthday, I thought at first it would be the same as ever.

The spirit willing but the flesh too weak.

Lord, his action was no stronger than a flower.

"Anne?" he cried, anxious.

"Yes," I lied, bored.

¶ Fifty-Six
Libels

It is time, I think, that I told you about the John Lane
libel.

> Why now?
> Because I say now, that's why.
> This is my book, and it comes as I write it.
> This is my story, as well as the story of me and Mr
> Shakespeare, and while I was playing the virginals this
> morning, as is my wont, I remembered that I had not yet
> told you about the John Lane libel, although I promised
> it as long ago as Chapter Eight.
> Here it is, then, without more ado.
> This is what happened. Listen carefully.

John Lane's a Stratford man, the son of the owner of
Alveston Manor, two miles up the Avon from here. There's
no love lost between the Lanes and the Shakespeares.

> Don't ask me why it started, but the feud goes back
> two generations.
> John Lane's grandfather Nicholas Lane, who was
> as rich as Crazes, once went out of his way to sue Mr
> Shakespeare's father for the price of a pig.
> John Lane's mother used to bite her thumb and
> pull faces behind the back of Mary Shakespeare, if ever she

saw that saintly woman in the market.

They're foul-mouthed and tiny-minded, the Family Lane.

John Lane, the youngest, is a Papist and a wine-bibber, like the rest.

You will recall that our Susanna was named for that heroine in the Apocrypha. The one who was falsely accused of immorality.

Well, so was my daughter falsely accused by this vile Lane.

It happened in the summer of 1613, after Mr Shakespeare had retired from the playhouses to live at home with me here, peacefully in Stratford.

At a public dinner, Lane got drunk.

Wine loosed his tongue, and out of his mouth came spewing wickedness.

Before falling, face-down, in the fish course, he was heard to blurt out that William Shakespeare's elder daughter had the running of the reins.

By the running of the reins he meant the pox.

Gonorrhea. The running of the kidneys.

Venereal disease. That's what he attributed to our Susanna.

(If you doubt me, you should consult the Alphabetical Table of Diseases which prefaces my good son-in-law John Hall's Select Observations on matters medical. The first entry under G is, "Gonorrhea, see running of the reins.")

And as if this was not enough, the despicable Lane then compounded his slander by turning his head sideways in the broiled salmon and declaring that Susanna had committed adultery with Ralph Smith at John Palmer's house.

*

None of which things is true.

It goes without saying.

The truth being that Susanna, then as now, is happily married, and the healthy mother of my grandchild Elizabeth.

The truth being that John Lane is a drunkard, and that wine makes bad men's tongues wag mad.

Sweet innocent Susanna!

Like her namesake, she brings out the worst in such swine as Lane, being witty and wise above her sex, so that they are consumed by a wicked need to bring her down to their own level.

Nobody believed what Lane said.

All the same, his filthy libels could not be let go unchallenged.

Reputation is important.

A good name is rather to be chosen than great riches (Proverbs, 22, i).

Take away someone's good name and you take away their life.

So Susanna, with her father's and my own approval, refuted the John Lane libel.

In July 1613 she brought an action for slander against him in the Ecclesiastical Court at Worcester Cathedral.

Principal witness for her was to be Robert Whatcott, who was later to be a witness of my husband's will. Whatcott had been sitting opposite Lane at table, and was prepared to swear that he had heard the offensive words.

But John Lane did not dare to come to court.

He lurked in hiding.

He put up no defence.

With a result that he lost the case, as he would have lost it anyway.

With a result that he was excommunicated.

With a result that now he sits by himself, and drinks, and drinks.

You may see him any day sitting drunkenly by the river Avon, abusing his own reflection among the swans.

He drinks also in Thomas Quiney's wine-shop, called The Cage, on the corner of High Street and Bridge Street.

His going in there makes relations between Susanna and Judith even more frosty, of course.

They seldom speak to each other. They deal with each other through me.

This affair did not curb John Lane's tongue.

He has been sued in Star Chamber for riot, and for libelling our vicar Thomas Wilson.

In court the churchwardens testified that he is a drunkard.

Quiney, I fear, is heading down that road too.

Yet observe good Dr Hall's decency, for despite all the difficulties between the two sisters he just treated Quiney for the scurvy with his Scorbutick Beer, and cured him.

I wish he had medicine to cure him of his drunkenness.

But such a herb has not been discovered, nor will it ever be.

The seed of that disease lies in men's hearts and souls. It is a malady of the spirit, and it is mortal.

Susanna says that in my husband's plays there are many libels against women and women's nature.

He either puts women on pedestals, insisting on

their absolute purity, or he fears and mistrusts them for their (usually imagined) infidelity.

In his world women are kept in bonds by men, either as virgin goddesses or as whores.

I say that he should have been dumped into the river with the dirty laundry for such things, dressed as a woman and beaten for his published pretence to potency, and pinched by fairies for his sinful lust and his manifold sins against love.

¶ Fifty-Seven
Sextus

When he had finished making that idle imperfect love, my husband Mr Shakespeare rolled over on his back on the gigantic bed.

He crossed his legs and scratched his knee-caps.

Did I tell you that he had uncommonly long arms?

Then, without so much as a by-your-leave, he started smoking this long pipe of tobacco.

It was a white clay pipe, and the weed was sweet-smelling.

I ate an apple and five Naples biscuits.

I lay there staring up at the canopy and the candles. There was black wax dripping down over those gross carvings.

To tell you the truth, those carvings reminded me of the images of the Last Judgement which there used to be on the walls of the Gild Chapel here at Stratford. They were whitewashed over when I was just a little girl, because they were too Popish. My father-in-law John Shakespeare, when he was Chamberlain, was responsible for that defacement.

I remember he used to boast that he got all the whitewashing done for two shillings.

But he died a Papist.
Human nature's complicated, isn't it?

I watched that black wax where it dripped and gathered.
    "This bed," I said. "How many sonnets did this bed cost?"
    I lay on my back stroking the sheets with the palms of my hands.
    The sheets felt smooth as butter.
    Mr Shakespeare did not flinch, though my question was rude.
    He sucked at his long pipe. He didn't bat an eyelid.
    "No sonnets," said he. "Just two poems."
    "Fancy!" I said. "Were they long then?"
    Sir Smile puffed, and nodded.
    "Longish," he said. "Look, I'll show you."

Then, setting his pipe aside, my husband went delving under one of the swansdown pillows. He looked as if he was swimming. He kicked his heels in the air. When he came out he was holding a book in each of his hands.
    They were a couple of slim gilt volumes, quarto size.
    He pressed them upon me, looking quite proud of himself.
    I only ever saw such books in a rich man's library.
    They were not like your penny broadsheets, your coney-catching pamphlets, or your cheap chapbooks.
    (Later, I learned that the regular editions of these books were more flimsy. These particular copies had been specially bound for my husband as a present from his patron.)
    Venus and Adonis, one of the books was called.

The other, *The Rape of Lucrece*.

Each book had the name William Shakespeare in bold print on its title page.

And each bore a dedication to the Right Honourable Henry Wriothesley, Earl of Southampton and Baron of Tichfield.

So that, I thought to myself, was how you spelt Rizley.

I made no remark about that, though.

I had no wish to be considered a bumpkin.

Instead:

"Venus," I said, "I know about. But who's this Lucrece?"

Mr Shakespeare reached for his clay pipe again.

"A Roman lady," he said.

"A Roman lady who got raped?" said I.

"Full marks," he said.

I bit into a fresh apple.

He started blowing smoke-rings.

I propped myself up on one elbow to watch his smoke-rings.

I have seen better.

"Who raped Lucrece?" I said.

"Another Roman," said Mr Shakespeare.

"Another Roman lady?" I asked him.

That made my husband cough.

"Of course not," he said. "A Roman man. A prince, as a matter of fact. One of the Tarquins. Sextus Tarquinius."

"Sextus," I said. "That's a nice name."

He frowned at me. "You think so?" He looked puzzled.

"Sextus," I said. "Yes. I like the sound of Sextus."

I was teasing him, of course.

I do not care two hoots for the _sound_ of words as a
general rule.

The sound of words is irrelevant to their sense.

Mr Shakespeare was a man for the sound of words.

I am a woman for their sense, and their sense only.

Meaning: that's what interests me, as it must
interest any other honest wife.

O yes, but I was teasing my husband with praise
of Sextus.

Mr Shakespeare, he did not get the point.

He could be slow on the uptake, when it suited him.

"Well," he told me, "that Sextus was a villain."

I smiled at the candles.

"No doubt," I said.

I munched some more apple.

I felt quite like Eve.

"But I still like the sound of his name," I told Mr
Shakespeare.

ℚ Fifty-Eight
Exile, Boars, and Nothing

It grew darker in the chamber.

Mr Shakespeare lay shaking his head, and sucking at his pipe.

But he soon found the pipe had gone out.

"So what happened to Lucrece?" I asked him. "I mean, after Sextus had raped her. . . ."

"She told her husband," my husband said. "Then she stabbed herself."

"And Sextus?" I asked him.

"He was driven into exile," Mr Shakespeare said.

I finished eating my apple, and then lay there licking my fingers.

"Is that all?" I said.

Mr Shakespeare fumbled with his tinderbox.

"What do you mean?" he demanded. "Is <u>what</u> all?"

"Exile," I said.

Mr Shakespeare frowned.

"It just seems a feeble sort of ending," I said. "Wouldn't it have been better to have had the husband kill your Sextus?"

"But he didn't," Mr Shakespeare protested. "You don't understand. The basis is historical. A true story."

I smiled my best smile at him.

"I thought poets were allowed to lie," I said.

I lay back then, and considered the burning candles.
I drummed with my heels a little on the bed.
"So who gets raped in the other one?" I said.

Mr Shakespeare dropped his match. "I beg your
pardon?"

"It's a straightforward question," I said. "Does
your Venus rape your Adonis or your Adonis rape your
Venus?"

I saw Mr Shakespeare start blushing at the thought
of Venus raping Adonis. He was remembering by
Welford millpool, no doubt. Or perhaps that other evening
under the great Charlecote oak.

"Of course," I went on quickly, feeling sorry for
him, "if it's purely historical, or – what's the right word?
– mythological, then –"

"My poems are not all rape," Mr Shakespeare
protested.

Well, I wasn't having that.

"Come on," I said. "Do me a favour. I know a bit
about that Venus story. It's the woman rapes the man in
that one, isn't it?"

Mr Shakespeare drew in air sharply through his
fine white nostrils.

Then he sighed.

His face was growing red.

"Venus is a goddess," he said. "She falls in love with
Adonis, a mortal. She detains him from the chase. She woos
him. But she cannot win his love."

Just like us, I thought. I had detained him from
the chase all right. He used to poach Lucy's deer in

Welford woods. And out at Charlecote too, when he got half a chance.

I was sure that Mr Shakespeare knew what I was thinking.

He could read me, as I've explained, like an open book.

So I didn't say a word of our affairs.

Instead:

"Promising," I said. "A good beginning and middle, but how does it end? Does Adonis go into exile?"

Mr Shakespeare's face was distorted.

He mumbled something.

"Beg pardon?" I said.

"He gets killed by a wild boar," my husband snapped.

I couldn't refrain from smiling.

I giggled.

Then I laughed out loud.

Well, I ask you.

What would you have done?

I threw back my head in the pillows, and I laughed and laughed.

Mr Shakespeare removed the clay pipe from his mouth and glared at me.

"What's so funny?" he demanded.

"I'm sorry," I said, controlling myself with an effort. "But your poems do sound just a little bit ridiculous. All rapes, or attempted rapes, then exile, boars, and nothing."

"Their plots are not important," Mr Shakespea; said earnestly. "It's the verse. It's what I make of the material. Let me just read you this passage –"

"I'd rather you didn't," I said. "I already have a headache."

¶ Fifty-Nine
Hellfire

I did not have a headache.

I was telling my poor artful husband a little white lie.

I did not have a headache.

It was just that I did not want to have to listen to his poesy.

Mr Shakespeare's recitation voice was golden, warm and gracious. It delighted the ear.

But it was not my ear that required delight at that time.

We lay side by side on the bed.

We lay side by side on those gorgeous smooth sheets, though not touching.

But I was naked.

And those candle flames now seemed like hellfire.

I did not have a headache.

It was strange.

This crazy conversation about the rape of Adonis and exile, boars, and nothing, had made me ache elsewhere.

All kinds of thoughts and images were racing through my head.

Lewd images.

Voluptuous thoughts.

Unspeakable things.

Some of these things, some of these thoughts and images, were comic.

The most compelling things were not comic at all.

I kept staring at the candles and the carvings.

The devils and the nymphs.

What they were doing.

I fancied that they moved.

I could see them at it.

That was a trick of the candlelight, no doubt.

But it was real enough that two of the candles had joined together, melting.

I watched the black wax where it dripped and gathered from these two candles twisted into one.

I just lay there, naked.

I kept stroking the black silk coverlet.

I fingered its stars.

They felt jagged and thick.

Holding stars in your hands can be bad for your head and your heart.

I could not turn to look at Mr Shakespeare.

I listened to his breathing.

His breathing was deep. But I knew he'd not fallen asleep.

Perhaps he was reading my mind again?

I don't know.

If I could tell you I would let you know.

If he was reading my mind, that might go some

way towards explaining the things that happened next.
     But my husband did not need to read my mind.

Because, before long, I said softly:
     "Henry Rizley."
     "Yes," said Mr Shakespeare.
     "Henry Rizley gave you this bed for those poems."
     "No. He gave me money. I bought the bed."
     "Money," I said.
     "Yes," he said.
     I hesitated.
     I still could not bring myself to look at Mr
Shakespeare.
     Then I realised that I was sniffing at the sheets.
     Face-down in the swansdown pillows, I was busy
sniffing at the sheets.
     "This bed," I said.
     My husband said nothing.
     "This bed," I whispered. "Has he slept in it?"

¶ *Sixty*
A Thousand Pounds

Mr Shakespeare would not answer.

So I knew.

*When Mr Shakespeare wouldn't answer, I knew
that his friend must have been in this bed where we were
now lying.*

"Jesus," I said. "Sweet merciful Jesus."

*I do not normally take the Lord's name lightly or
in vain.*

*It pains me now to have to recall and record that
I said "Jesus" like that.*

But I must tell it as it happened.

I don't lie.

*And telling you the truth means including the
deeds and the sayings which will do me no credit when the
trumpet sounds and the Last Judgement is called.*

I could not take my eyes off those two candles.

"What do men do?" I whispered.

There was no reply.

*But I heard my husband draw his breath sharply,
as if he was in pain.*

I whispered:

"Good, is it?"

I felt the bed shift.

I turned and looked.

Mr Shakespeare was standing up.

He was taking off the lambskin jacket.

Then he reached out for one of those ropes and closed the curtains of the bed all around us.

"Rizley," I said. "Earl of Southampton. Baron of Tichfield."

That bed was now like a room within the room.

A secret place.

"Money," I said. "You whore," I said.

The wax dripped down from the headboard. It was staining the sheets.

There was a hot drop of it on one of the swansdown pillows. It sizzled the silk.

I whispered:

"How much did he give you?"

My husband muttered something.

"How much?" I said.

Then Mr Shakespeare spoke it clear and coldly.

"He gave me a thousand pounds," Mr Shakespeare said.

¶ Sixty-One
Fact

I stared at Mr Shakespeare.

Mr Shakespeare did not smile.

He was looking hard at me.

"What did you do?" I breathed. "What did you do that was worth a thousand pounds?"

Mr Shakespeare was naked now.

His member stood up stiff as any poker.

"You want to know," he said. "You really want to know."

It wasn't a question.

It was a statement of fact.

"I want to know," I whispered. "What did you do?"

"Why, I buggered him, my dear," Mr Shakespeare said softly.

"And what is that?" I enquired. "What does it mean?"

Mr Shakespeare answered nothing.

His eyes were like burning coals.

He was biting his lip.

When he stopped biting his lip, he kissed me hard on my lips. Then he stroked my cheeks with his fingers and kissed me gently on the eyelids.

Once my husband had kissed me on my eyelids, I chose to keep my eyes shut, and I waited.

I felt Mr Shakespeare move behind me.

I felt the bed shift as he knelt upon it.

I could feel him crouched behind me in the dark.

His hands came down and he clasped my hips tight from behind.

Then I felt his engorged member smack-smacking at my bottom cheeks.

"She wants to know," he said coldly. "I do believe she really wants to know."

His voice sounded far away. But I could feel him hot and hard between my bottom cheeks.

"I do!" I cried eagerly. "Yes, please, I do! How do you do it?"

Then:

"Like this," said Mr Shakespeare.

And then he did it to me.

Sixty-Two
Snails

It hurt me at first.

Then it didn't hurt.

Hurt me or not, once Mr Shakespeare had started there was no stopping him.

"Good?" he cried. "Like it?"

"No!" I cried. "No, I don't, no, I won't, no, no. . . ."

But, then, after some more of it:

"Yes!"

Snails were Mr Shakespeare's favourite creatures.

I once saw him sit and watch a snail on a stalk for an hour, approving the way it shrank into its shell when its horns touched the leaf.

¶ Sixty-Three
Again

*When we had done, Mr Shakespeare started talking
about the money.*

That bed had not cost so very much, he said.

*He had plenty of the thousand pounds left
over.*

*He was going to buy shares in a new playhouse
which Mr Burbage was building on the Bankside.*

*His plays would be performed there, my husband
said.*

*That way he would get paid for the plays, and also
receive a percentage of their profits.*

Money made money, Mr Shakespeare said.

Soon he would purchase property as well.

*The day would come, my clever husband promised,
when we would live in the finest house in Stratford. . . .*

(Well, it didn't.

We had to settle for the second-best.)

I grew tired of his talking.

So I touched him.

*"You want it again?" Mr Shakespeare asked
wonderingly. "You want it again up there?"*

I wanted it.

I wanted it again up there.

And Mr Shakespeare proved more than willing to give it to me where and how I wanted it.

I fell asleep at last.
     I fell asleep worn out by what he'd done to me.
     A very great peace came over me.
     I do not think I was ever so pleased or contented.
     It started to rain as I fell asleep, I remember that.
     I could hear the April rain falling gently upon the roof.
     Mr Shakespeare was still talking about the money as I fell asleep.
     But it was not about the money that I dreamt.

Sixty-Four
My Dream

I dreamt I was up on Stinchcombe Hill among the foxgloves.

Foxgloves I love.

There is no blatancy about the beauty of foxgloves, nor any great blaze of light as when the ox-eye daisies wave over the fields in June.

There is a something subtle about foxgloves.

There is mind-rest. There is balm in the depths of a foxglove bell.

I dreamt that I lifted a foxglove and looked right into it. I dreamt that I went into it, delighting in the splashes and the markings, the fine filaments and the silken texture of the flower, the pink and the purple and the crimson, the dark brown and the white, the poise of the stalk, the droop of the bells.

I think perhaps I dreamt I was a foxglove.

Sixty-Five
Donkey's Head

Next morning I was woken by this braying.

I looked about in the sweet fishy gloom of the chamber.

I saw the Devil standing at the foot of that bed.

"He-haw!" brayed the Devil. "He-haw!"

The Devil was stark naked save for this donkey's head.

"He-haw!" he brayed again. Then: "Ha! Haw!"

At the same time, I heard singing from the street below.

The words of the song were lovely.

I found them later in a book of airs.

The song went like this:

FAIN WOULD I CHANGE THAT NOTE
TO WHICH FOND LOVE HATH CHARMED ME,
LONG, LONG TO SING BY ROTE
FANCYING THAT THAT HARMED ME.
YET WHEN THIS THOUGHT DOTH COME,
LOVE IS THE PERFECT SUM
OF ALL DELIGHT;
I HAVE NO OTHER CHOICE

EITHER FOR PEN OR VOICE
TO SING OR WRITE.

O LOVE, THEY WRONG THEE MUCH
THAT SAY THY SWEET IS BITTER;
WHEN THY RIPE FRUIT IS SUCH
AS NOTHING CAN BE SWEETER.
FAIR HOUSE OF JOY AND BLISS,
WHERE TRUEST PLEASURE IS,
I DO ADORE THEE:
I KNOW THEE WHAT THOU ART,
I SERVE THEE WITH MY HEART
AND FALL BEFORE THEE.

It was the wet fishmonger.

It must have been that fishmonger who was singing.

It was a lovely song.

Remembrance of it still brings tears into my eyes, and sends a little shiver down my spine.

Meanwhile, as I listened to that singing, the Devil's member was thrusting out towards me.

I recognised the Devil by his member.

It looked like a spear.

It was shaking.

I couldn't stop myself. I reached out for that little shaking devil's spear.

I reached out to hold and stroke the Devil's upright member.

Then I rolled over on my belly and knelt up on that bed.

I directed the Devil's member where I wanted it.

"He-haw!" brayed the Devil. "Ha! Whore!" cried

the Devil. "Can't get enough of it now, can she?"

   Mr Shakespeare buggered me wearing his donkey's head.

My husband.
   Lion-hearted Mr Shakespeare.
   The tender ass.

¶ Sixty-Six
46

O little book of mine, here is something very different for your keeping.

O Reader, my friend, here is something somewhat else for you to do.

Take out your Bible.

Turn to the Psalms.

Count the 46th word from the start of the 46th Psalm.

Read that word aloud.

Now count the 46th word from the end of the same 46th Psalm, omitting the final Selah.

Read that word aloud, also.

The two words are:

SHAKE and SPEAR.

My husband Mr Shakespeare saw to that. Or so he told me, and would have had me believe.

It happened, so my clever husband said, like this.

In the last stages of the preparation of the Authorised Version of the Bible, done at King James's direction, the committee responsible gave out a few passages of the Old Testament to be looked over by eminent literary men of the day.

Mr Shakespeare was given some of the Psalms.

This would have been in the springtime of 1610, the year before my husband retired here to Stratford.

He was then, I dare say, at the height of his fame.

And so it came about, as he told me later, that on his 46th birthday he found himself required to polish (as he put it) the new English version of the 46th Psalm, "To the chief Musician for the sons of Korah, A Song upon Alamoth."

Which my husband dutifully did, then inserting his own name into it, in two halves, so that no one would readily notice it, as a kind of secret signature, in the manner described.

Is this story true?

Did Mr Shakespeare really do that?

Or did he notice in an idle moment that the Psalmist's words fell out like that in the King James Bible (which he knew I loved), and then make up for my benefit this tale of his being responsible?

I cannot say for certain.

But on the whole I must say that it seems to me less likely that he might have constructed the tale upon the coincidence of the words than that he might have been responsible for the words being there in the first place in the manner he claimed.

He liked to play with words, as I have told you. (Remember that sonnet in my Chapter Thirty-Five and what he did in it with the name Hathaway.)

And he liked to celebrate his own birthday in perverse ways. (Memory of mortality always brought out some sly imp in him.)

So his fooling with Psalm 46 on his 46th birthday would assuredly be quite in keeping with his fooling with me, his wife, on his thirtieth, on this day that I can't forget no matter what I do, and that's the simple truth of it.

My husband.
　　　　Psalming Mr Shakespeare.
　　　　The arsy-versy man.

¶ Sixty-Seven
As I Liked It

Thus, friends, I have to come back to that bed.

I have to return to those embroidered swansdown pillows below the melting black candles.

For I have still to tell you the rest of it.

I've told you the start of it, but I have still to tell you what followed.

What he did.

What I did.

What he said.

What I said.

What we made of it.

Since what followed the first unnatural act was in no sense mere epilogue.

What followed the act was the meaning.

No less.

Am I right?

I am.

And I should know, shouldn't I?

For I am one to whom meaning is all.

I must endeavour, my dears, to give you the gist of that meaning.

Though I might say that I cannot claim to comprehend completely what it encompasses.

It's like Daniel and that vision of the ram and the goat.

And it came to pass, when I, even I Daniel, had seen the vision, and sought for the meaning, then, behold, there stood before me as the appearance of a man (Daniel, 8, xv).

Only I can't expect any angel Gabriel coming to explain our meaning for me.

Well, even if that bed has employment now in a nunnery, I say it would blush if it could talk and tell you all the strange sweet cardinal things that we did in it.

My husband Mr Shakespeare had compared it to a playhouse.

Amen, say I.

So it was.

That bed was a private playhouse where we acted out together his dreams and his fantasies.

For Mr Shakespeare, remember, was a man who could get drunk on moonlight. He lived by dreams. His dreams dreamed him.

O, and I was a willing accomplice in what happened in that bed, a most wanton actress.

What we did was always as I liked it.

Don't think otherwise for a moment.

Mr Shakespeare never forced himself upon me.

What we did was as I wanted it.

Because now I had found out that I liked what he liked.

Because now I had discovered that I wanted what he wanted.

Liked it? Wanted it?

I confess that I adored it.

Reader, I doted on the act.

And all our various secret plays had that one same carnal ending.

¶ Sixty-Eight
The Acts

Often I dressed as a boy and Mr Shakespeare dressed himself up in my clothes.

I liked to wear doublet and hose for my husband's delight.

It amused me to fumble in the folds of my own petticoats in quest of his member.

We loved to watch ourselves in the looking-glass while we garbed and disported ourselves thus.

I would help him to put on my stockings.

He would chase me and spank me and make me wear his boots.

Mr Shakespeare had costumes as well in a brass-bound trunk he kept under the bed.

Gowns, crowns, masks, wigs, skulls, daggers, and suchlike.

Sometimes we used these props.

But mostly not.

Usually just words were sufficient to get us going.

Such words!

His words.

A bee's sting pricks the deepest, when it is full of honey.

Mr Shakespeare would start talking as he lit the long black candles.

Then he'd pull the curtains around us and shut out the real world, him still talking, talking, and we'd act out his dreams.

Once he made me believe that the bed was an enchanted island floating in the sea.
   I was the daughter of this magician who ruled over the island.
   The magician was named Prosperous.
   Miranda, he called me.
   Mr Shakespeare called himself someone or something called Caliban.
   Caliban had very beastly lusts.

Then I had to be this shrew called Kate Sly and he was some peculiar Veronese gentleman, one Petruchio, whose pleasure it was to tame me of my shrewishness.
   Guess how. . . .

Then I was a Duke's daughter who ran away and lived in a forest called Arden (which was Mr Shakespeare's mother's maiden name). I had to dress as a man to be safe in the forest, but my husband became a country wench who fell in love with me.
   This one got complicated before Mr Shakespeare solved all our confusions with his pintle.

Then I was Tit something or other, the Queen of the Fairies, and Mr Shakespeare was a plausible weaver, rude, vigorous, and stupid, who came upon me on a moonlit bank.
   It was, he said, midsummer.
   He had me lie face down among the pillows.
   I smelt them.
   I bit them.

The smell was just-baked bread.

The taste was deathly sweet as lavender.

"Why do you get so hard?" I said. "You get so hard."

And he, as he came, cried:

"Oh, extreme, extreme!"

I remember that strange saying. He cried it out as if he was in pain.

But it was never pain, I'm sure.

It was pure pleasure.

Another time I was the Queen of the Goths, Queen Tamora, and he was a Roman named Titus who killed my two sons and baked their remains in a pie.

That was a nasty one.

I didn't much care for that one.

Because he got a real pie, an eel-pie.

He bought it down in Turnagain Lane and he made me eat it with him sitting up on the bed.

I was nearly sick.

It was not the eel that made me feel sick, it was the idea that it was not eel.

But I ate it.

You see, I wanted Mr Shakespeare.

By the time he'd finished talking I needed him to do what I knew he would do when we'd eaten that pie.

And he did do it.

Twice.

Then, another peculiar one, when I was this Italian girl, very young, Juliet he called me, and I had to pretend that I was lying dead in a tomb (that bed!) from a potion given to me by a Papist friar.

And Mr Shakespeare was my lover, name of

Romeo, and when this Romeo thought his little Juliet was dead he went and drank rat poison.

Only Juliet was not dead.

The friar had only given her a sleeping potion.

So when I woke from my trance I saw Romeo's body lying there beside me and I had to act out seizing his dagger and killing myself for grief.

I had to stab myself in the little bosom just for grief of Romeo.

Then Mr Shakespeare kissed his dead little Juliet and did that other thing to her.

Then he made me some wicked queen whose name I forget walking in my sleep and trying to wash imaginary blood-stains from my hands.

My husband the king was womanish.

But I had stirred him up to murder for the crown.

And, when it came to it, he managed to do the man's part.

So did Mr Shakespeare.

Then, another night, I was the lady-love of a Prince of Denmark.

The Prince of Denmark went mad, or pretended to go mad, or went mad with pretending to go mad, I could not determine which, and neither I think could Mr Shakespeare, but anyway I had to wander about the room singing and strewing imagined flowers and then act out that I had strayed to the banks of a stream and drowned myself.

At this point my husband cried out that I was actually Katherine Hamlet, a poor unfortunate who was drowned in the Avon near Stratford when he was a boy.

That bed was the stream.

Mr Shakespeare jumped into it after me.

I might say that he had me drown face-downwards.
Which is, of course, quite contrary to nature.

Then he was a blackamoor soldier called Othello in the
service of the Venetian state.
    And he smothered me with a pillow on the bed
because I was his wife and he'd been worked up to believe
that I'd been unfaithful to him with his lieutenant.
    Mr Shakespeare made up a lovely bit of a song for
that one, when we were doing what I knew we'd do after
the smothering.
    Something about a weeping willow, that song.
    That and the other activity brought tears to my
eyes, I do remember.

And then I was Cleopatra of Egypt with a make-believe
snake.
    (I don't think this had much to do with our cat.)
    I had to call that snake my baby.
    I had to say it sucked me to sleep as its teeth were
dispatching me.

And, another time, Mr Shakespeare was Antiochus or
something, the King of Antioch anyway, and I was his
daughter; and another I was three daughters, and he was
an old British king called King Leir. . . .

But I shall not speak of those ones –
    Enough.
    Or too much!

Sixty-Nine
Hatted Kit

In case it was too much, here is an antidote.

A something sweet to settle the head and the heart.

It is my excellent pudding recipe for:

HATTED KIT
(A Very Old Warwickshire Dish)

Warm slightly over the fire two pints of buttermilk.

Pour it into a dish and carry it to the side of a cow.

Milk into it about one pint of milk, having previously put into the dish sufficient rennet for the whole.

After allowing it to stand for a while, lift the curd, place it on a sieve, and press the whey through until the curd is quite stiff.

Season with sugar and nutmeg before serving, whip some thick cream, season it also with a little grated nutmeg and sugar and mix gently with the curd.

This dish can quite well be made without

milking the cow into it, although in my experience
direct milking always puts a better hat on the kit.

This, I need hardly add, was one of Mr Shakespeare's
favourite puddings.

Seventy
The Case

Infinite riches in a little room. . . .

    That's how my husband Mr Shakespeare described what we got up to.

    "Infinite riches in a little room," he said somewhat coldly, standing with his back to the window, watching me on the bed, the while he drank tobacco smoke from his white clay pipe.

    I couldn't put it any better, myself.

Not that this was his own phrase.

    I used to think it was.

    But I've found out different.

    I quoted it one day in an innocent context, and my learned daughter Susanna instructed me that it is a phrase which comes from the works of another playwright, a rival poet.

    A young man called Christopher Marlowe, the son of a Canterbury cobbler.

    An atheist, Susanna says. And another who loved tobacco and young boys, so people say.

    This Marlowe was murdered in a brawl in a tavern in Deptford. A man called Frizer stabbed him through the eyes, Susanna told me.

I believe my husband might have known this Marlowe.

He mixed, in London, in some very low company, after all, so I cannot put this beyond the realms of possibility, alas.

Most certainly Mr Shakespeare must have known this Marlowe's work.

He knew it well enough to lift that line about *infinite riches in a little room* and pass it on to me as suitable for describing what we got up to that week we spent in his lodgings above the wet fishmonger's on the corner of Turnagain Lane, by St Helen's church, Bishopsgate.

Whether it was him or the atheist Marlowe who coined the phrase does not matter two hoots.

Infinite riches in a little room.

It fits the case, doesn't it?

My husband.

Bright-eyed Mr Shakespeare.

The magpie man.

¶ Seventy-One
Other Events of April, 1594

*What other things were happening that springtime of 1594
while we were at it there?*

What events were taking place in the wide world?

*I looked it all up in a budget of news which cousin
Greene loaned to me.*

*Here are a few of the more important public
happenings which I found.*

4th April. A PLOT TO KILL THE QUEEN.
*A man called Polwhele came over to London from Calais
to give information to Lord Treasurer Burleigh that one
Captain Jacques, a soldier from Sir William Stanley's
company, had a design to kill Her Majesty the Queen.
This Jacques, Polwhele said, had several times urged him
to come to England to murder the Queen, and on his
refusing Jacques said that the end of a soldier was but
beggary, to be killed with a bullet and thrown into a
ditch, and to take such a matter in hand would be glorious
before God, the Queen being a wicked creature, and likely
to overthrow all Christendom. Jacques directed him how
to get to England safely, and what speeches to use to the
Lord Treasurer if intercepted, saying that if he himself
could go to England, the killing of the Queen would be the*

first thing he would do. Polwhele also drew in two other men, John Annias and Patrick Collen, an Irish soldier, with having come to England to kill the Queen. Both were taken and lodged separately in prison.

6th April. A PLOT TO BURN THE TOWER.

John Daniel, another Irishman, told Mr Justice Young of a plot for the firing of the Tower of London. He declared that there was a vault where brimstone and gunpowder had been laid, and near to it a trapdoor often open. It was purposed that two men like labourers should come in as though they were workmen in the Tower, and cast bales into the vault where the brimstone was so that in a short time it should take fire and consume all. Further, this Daniel reported that there was a device to set the ships at Billingsgate on fire, and the houses also; and then to set the inns and woodstacks on fire in London.

16th April. DEATH OF THE EARL OF DERBY.

The young Earl of Derby, Ferdinando Stanley, died at Latham on April the 16th, having been sick of some strange sickness for eleven days. Outwardly his diseases were vomiting of sour or rusty matter with blood, the yellow jaundice, melting of his fat, swelling and hardness of his spleen, a vehement hiccough, and, for four days before he died, stopping of his water. All these were caused in the opinion of his physicians partly by surfeit, partly by the excessive exercise that he took for four days together in Easter week. In all the time of his sickness, which began on the 5th April and continued until he died, he often took Beza's stone and Unicorn's horn; his pulse was always good but his strength indifferent, the number of his vomits being fifty-two and of his stools twenty-nine. The Earl's death was so unaccountable that many began to suspect he had been bewitched. In the beginning of his sickness he had strange dreams. On the 10th April, Mr Halsall, one of his gentlemen, found in my lord's chamber about midnight an image of wax with hair in colour like his hair twisted round the belly. This image was spotted and soon after spots appeared also upon the Earl's sides and belly. Mr Halsall hastily cast the image in the fire before it was viewed by others, thinking that by burning it he should relieve his lord of the witchcraft and burn the witch who so much tormented him. But unhappily it fell out the contrary for after the melting of the image the Earl declined.

A homely woman about the age of fifty years was found mumbling in a corner of his chamber. She seemed often to ease his lordship both of vomiting and hiccough, but it was noted that whenever he was so eased she herself was much troubled in the same way, and the matter which she vomited was like that which passed from him. But at the last, one of the Earl's doctors, spying her tempering and blessing the juice of certain herbs, tumbled her pot down and rated her from the chamber. The Earl himself cried out in all his sickness that the doctors laboured in vain because he was assuredly bewitched. During this last illness the Bishop of Chester and his chaplain, Mr Lee, were with him.

21st April. THE CONFESSION OF HUGH CAHILL.
Hugh Cahill, another Irishman, voluntarily confessed before the interrogator Richard Topcliffe that when he was at Brussels he heard one Father Holt and others say it would be a most blessed thing to kill the Queen, as by doing it a man would win Heaven, and become a saint if he should be killed. He that should do it would be chronicled for ever, this priest told Cahill.

Cahill was then advised to go to Court, and serve someone about the Queen's privy chamber, and then to waylay Her Majesty in some progress and kill her with a sword and a dagger at a gate or narrow passage, or as she walked in one of her galleries. They promised him *100* crowns towards his charges, and *2000* more to be paid when he had killed her, and his pension augmented from *15* crowns a month to £*30*.

23rd April. BRUNO IMPOUNDED.

Abroad, in Rome, a philosopher called Giordano Bruno was impounded by the Inquisition, his crime being that he had claimed that the earth goes round about the sun. (They burnt him for this heresy six years later.)

WEATHER NEWS.

All that month of April there were great storms of wind, that overturned trees and steeples, barns and houses. In Beaulieu forest in Worcestershire many oaks were uprooted, and on the Thursday before Palm Sunday more than fifteen hundred trees came down in Horton Wood. In the town of Stafford the steeple was thrown down, and a thousand pounds' worth of damage was done to the church roof. In Cankewood more than three thousand trees were overthrown by the storms, and some fifty other steeples fell in different parts of the country.

OTHER NEWS IN BRIEF.

The English were sacking the Portuguese colony of Pernambuco, King Henry IV of France was entering Paris, King Philip II of Spain was closing the port of Lisbon to Dutch shipping, the Turks were recapturing the fortress of Raab, and Sir John Burgh was slain in a duel at Charing Cross by Mr John Gilbert. The executions of

*the traitors Lopez, Ferrara, and Tinoco were postponed
until June, by the Queen's command.*

Enough of history.
    So much for the wide world.
    *Meanwhile, my dears, in that little room above the
fishmonger's. . . .*

¶ Seventy-Two
Philosophy of the Act

Contra Natura. . . .

That's what I read somewhere as an opinion of what we were doing.

That particular act, the pursuit of self-gratification against Nature, contra Natura, the writer said, is the ultimate sin, because it denies the whole purpose and meaning of love.

Nothing drags the soul down more, this man said.

According to him, it was the sin against Nature, as well as the sin against grace.

Well, I ask you.

Reader, is that sound religion?

I admit there is none that I ever dared to question in the matter.

My mind says it might be.

My heart and my body cry No!

Mr Shakespeare himself talked a streak on the subject, when he wasn't busy doing it.

Let me try and remember something of what he then said.

Let me try and recall for you my husband Mr Shakespeare's philosophy of the act.

He said its meaning was it had no meaning.

He said its meaning was it had no meaning most when the act was done by a man and a woman.

A man doing it to a man was nothing much, he said.

A man doing it to a woman was all, he said.

To tell you the truth now, I was bored by his talk. But I asked my husband what he meant by "all".

Then Mr Shakespeare said that by "all" he meant that the act when done by a man and a woman was a chosen pleasure, a pure joy, the extreme of sense.

And, more than that, he said, it was a meaning nothing that was escape from meaning.

It was an escape from personality, he said.

I did not understand this.

I say the meaning was pleasure.

The pleasure only was the meaning for me.

I suspect that for Mr Shakespeare pleasure was never sufficient.

I suspect that for that reason he had to invent other reasons for liking what he liked.

I suspect also that in fact he favoured this particular act of love because its wrongness corresponded to his own.

(Remember Bidford and Wilmcote!

See page 66.)

For my part, I enjoyed the act also in that it removed the fear of child-bearing.

It was an improvement on crocodile dung as a means of contraception.

Perhaps, for Mr Shakespeare's part, he enjoyed it in that it removed the risk of child-giving.

He never spoke of that, though.

He did speak of liking it, in the context of

child-conceiving, in that it could be a wilder and a more abandoned act than the common way of a man with a woman.

Extreme, was the word he favoured.

Also he spoke of liking it expressly because it was forbidden.

Forbidden acts of dark unmeaning held great glamour for my husband Mr Shakespeare.

I could not say why.

I remember that one night he spoke of some ancient abomination of magicians called the Cathars, or the Bulgars, whom other people called The Perfect Ones, and he told me that they especially had favoured what we did.

I did not care for such talk.

I admit that I hardly listened to what he then said.

It seemed to me that Mr Shakespeare wanted his pursuit of unmeaning to verge on the Satanic.

I hated and I hate all that.

I say now that I reject it.

What we did, I say, had nothing to do with magic.

I did what we did because I liked it.

I only wanted to have him do it to me, not to talk about it.

When Mr Shakespeare talked too much, I tempted him with my bottom.

That shut him up.

It was on the second last night that he danced his spider dance.

I gave it that name.

I called it his spider dance.

Our love-making ended, "I would like now to dance, wife," said he.

"Very well, husband. You may dance to your heart's content," I told him.

(I had no desire to dance with him, recalling that time I tried to teach him the lavolta.)

Mr Shakespeare danced on his own, up and down the chamber, naked.

His pintle looked like one of those long purples, dead men's fingers.

The dance was a thing of whirling arms, high-kicking legs, grotesque capers and coy grimaces.

He threw his legs high and whirled his long arms as he capered.

His shadow upon the rafters was like a second dancing spider, about to tup him.

"You look like David," I said. "Leaping and dancing before the ark of the Lord."

And David danced before the Lord with all his might; and David was girded with a linen ephod.

So David and all the house of Israel brought up the ark of the Lord with shouting, and with the sound of the trumpet.

And as the ark of the Lord came into the city of David, Michal Saul's daughter looked through a window, and saw king David leaping and dancing before the Lord; and she despised him in her heart.

(2 Samuel, 6, xiv–xvi)

Only I might say that I never despised Mr Shakespeare.

Not even when he fell into the Shottery mill-race and came out all damp, green, and soft like the down on the cheek of a peach.

Not even when he rolled home, drunk and empty-eyed, after that last fatal night with his poet-friends from London.

"Hullo," I said then. "Anybody in?"

I'd got a feeling in my water.

I knew that he was dying.

But I did not scold or nag him. And I never did despise him.

"Hullo," I said then. "Anybody in?"

With that the scritch-owl cried, and soon enough the night raven sat croaking hard by his window.

"Jesu have mercy upon me," Mr Shakespeare said.

And therewithal my husband laid him down in his bed, from whence he never rose again.

¶ Seventy-Three
Lilies

All good things must come to an end.

Am I right?

I am.

The week passed quickly.

It was on the last night in that bed that I said to Mr Shakespeare, keeping my voice as flat and my tone as casual as I could:

"What's he like then? Tell me."

"Who?" he demanded.

"You know who," I said. "Your friend. That Rizley."

My husband smiled.

"You little whore," said he.

Mr Shakespeare seemed to like the idea of his wife being a whore.

He touched me as he said it.

We lay naked, side by side, between the sheets.

His pintle stood up like a tent-pole against the silk coverlet.

He was smiling, Sir Smile, soft as shit and twice as nasty, and he touched me between my legs, when he said I was a whore.

There was a smell as if the glue-pot had come
unstuck.
I smiled back sweetly.
"Well, it takes one to know one, doesn't it?" I
reminded him.

He was that sly, Mr Shakespeare.
I should know, shouldn't I?
If he could have, he would have said no more.
As I live and breathe, I know he would have preferred
to keep his secrets.
But I wasn't having that.
Not on your life, Reader.
Besides, since he was looking at me now as if he could
eat me without salt I knew there was a chance to make him
talk.
"Come on," I said, stretching. "Don't be such
a spoil-sport. You can't really expect me to turn tail
and go home knowing nothing about this rival of mine
except that he is rich and his name is Henry
Rizley."
"He's not your rival," Mr Shakespeare said.
"But you do do it with him, don't you?" I
demanded.
Mr Shakespeare sighed.
Then he shrugged.
Then he withdrew his hand from my lap, sniffing
at it craftily as he tickled his little moustache with a
half-bent finger.
He insisted once more that the meaning of the
favoured act was quite different with me.
"But what's he like, your Rizley?" I persisted.
My husband started biting his well-bitten
fingernails.

He was mumbling something through this small meal of his hand.

"Come again," I requested.

"Sonnets," muttered Mr Shakespeare. "I suppose I could let you read the sonnets I wrote about him."

Well, thank you for nothing, thought I.

What a pawky fox he was!

"That's cheating, dear husband," I told him. "You know I can't stand poesy."

"I know you don't want to understand it," Mr Shakespeare said.

"Can't stand, won't understand," said I. "Just tell me in plain words is all I ask. I don't want sonnets. Keep sonnets for those who need sugar the same as you. What's he look like, this noble friend of yours, my rival?"

Mr Shakespeare stopped biting his fingernails.

Now he was rubbing his little belly as if he felt an ulcer coming on.

Then he frowned and said:

"The strange thing is. . . ."

He stopped.

"Go on," I prompted.

Mr Shakespeare reached out with his hand again.

He started stroking my hair where we lay among the pillows in the candlelight.

This I had not anticipated.

This was very nice.

"Perhaps it is not strange at all," my husband murmured.

"Strange or not, tell me!"

"Well, he's just about the opposite of you," Mr Shakespeare said.

These words seemed to deny what his hand was doing.

I could have been angry.

Instead, I said:

"Ah, yes, forgive me. I was forgetting. How could I forget it? How did you allow me to forget it? He's summer to my winter, isn't he?"

My husband touched a finger to my lips.

"I didn't mean that," he said gently. "That is not what I meant."

"O, rocks!" said I. "Tell us in plain words. Just describe him! Leave me out of it, will you, please? But just tell me what Rizley is like!"

So he did, Mr Shakespeare.

He just told me what Rizley was like.

A lovely boy, Mr Shakespeare said, with a fair complexion.

Twenty-one summers old, Mr Shakespeare said, and a rose-cheeked Adonis.

His breath sweeter than violets, Mr Shakespeare said.

His hair like the amber buds of marjoram, my husband added.

An angel, he said.

A spirit, he said.

A saint, he said.

So he said, Mr Shakespeare.

So he said, so he said.

My husband.

Pathetic Mr Shakespeare.

The love-sick fool.

Well, I ask you.

Women are not angels, though they have angels' faces.

Even less may men be.

I yawned, then.

I couldn't help it.

I covered my mouth with my hand.

"You make him sound too good to be true," I told Mr Shakespeare. "I'm sorry, but what is he, an Easter lily?"

My husband looked wounded.

"The day must come when you find out different," I warned him. "Lilies that fester smell far worse than weeds. Just remember that."

He was staring at me, dumb-found.

Tears came to his eyes.

He blinked, and the tears fell down his face.

I watched those slow tears trickle.

Then I kissed him.

In that moment, I think, I most loved him.

There was never a time when I did not love Mr Shakespeare, let me say that, not from our beginning to his ending, nor has there ever been such a loveless time since.

But in that moment when he wept at the prospect of his own necessary disenchantment with another I do believe I loved my husband most.

Then:

"Welcome to the Netherlands!" I whispered.

And thus without too much difficulty I led my husband Mr Shakespeare to think and to feel that I had lost all interest in the subject of lilies.

Seventy-Four
(Untitled)

O little book, you are nearly all used up.

I have only six pages of you left to me after the present page.

O dear little book of mine, I shall miss my writing in you.

O my darling dear, what shall I do when I have done with you?

My sad, my saddest story, is all told, almost. . . .

O little book, I know that one day someone reading you may say:

"So that's why her husband left her for all those years!"

Meaning: Mr Shakespeare went away to escape from the sound of his wife's voice.

My stories.

My proverbs.

My nagging wisdom.

My talkative truth.

My unstoppable, ungainsayable woman's voice.

To that Reader, as to all other good Readers, may I say:

Yes, but Mr Shakespeare needed me.

First he needed me to flee from. Then he needed me to return to.

My husband came back home to Stratford, don't ever forget.

After this key time in London, he always came back home every year, for his birthday, when he could.

Then, in the April of 1611, the year when the King James Bible was published, Mr Shakespeare came back home to me for good, and he spent the last five years of his life with me here where he started from.

I was his Alpha and Omega, his beginning and his ending, his mother, his bride, and his layer-out.

He was born at my hands.

He came alive in my backside.

Reader, he died in my arms.

Seventy-Five
Endings

"*Your eyes,*" *he declared, "are nothing like the sun.*"

"*Oh thanks!*" *I said.*

It was the morning of the day I left my husband Mr William Shakespeare's London lodgings, in that long-ago April of 1594 which is still just like yesterday in my mind.

I was looking at my own face in the looking-glass.

What did I see?

I saw white parchment cheeks and an ivory-white forehead.

I saw hair like black wire.

I saw two pitch-ball eyes, two sloes, two eyes raven-black, like mourners.

I looked into that glass and what did I see?

I saw a woman coloured ill looking back at me.

My husband Mr Shakespeare came and stood behind my shoulder.

"*Nothing like the sun,*" *he said again, earnestly, nibbling the while on a little twisted stick of sugar candy.*

"*Understand this,*" *he went on, "I mean to compliment you with the truth. Poets, as you've often told me, lie. They make far-fetched comparisons. I am just being truthful for once. You are worth the truth, Anne."*

I smiled to myself.

I smiled also at the liar in the mirror.

Sir Smile, he smiled back.

He seemed to be offering me another of his special smiles, pulling down his top lip to flatten the little hole in the middle which is where my mother told me the guardian angel leaves the heavenly thumb-print as we come into this world.

It was a handsome smile.

But whether Mr Shakespeare smiled at me or to himself I never could determine.

When she was small my cat Egypt was much delighted to play with her image in a glass.

I was thinking of that as I sat there and looked in my mirror.

Cats will after kind, as they say, always.

But I was not a kitten any more.

I was painting my pale lips.

Then I rouged my death-pale cheeks.

I observed:

"The truth is I look worn-out, and no wonder."

I did.

And it wasn't.

It had been such a sweet little orgy of a week!

I started brushing my hair then, but my husband took the hairbrush from my hand.

Mr Shakespeare brushed my hair for me.

He played with each long dark tress, drawing the hair out tight, staring in the looking-glass at our two reflections.

Mr Shakespeare brushed it quick and he brushed it slow, he brushed it hard and he brushed it soft, until my hair was shining like ebony in the early morning sunlight that fell through the attic window.

"In the old days," Mr Shakespeare said, "black was not counted fair."

"I can't help being a brunette," I said.

"As black as hell," Mr Shakespeare said, brushing. "As dark as night."

"There you go again," I said. "Far-fetched comparisons! The lies of poesy! I'm a woman, not a devil, and you know it."

I stood up.

Well, I ask you.

What would you have done?

It was time to go.

It was time to go and get on with the rest of my life.

I never could abide a long goodbye.

It irked me, therefore, when at the door to the stairway, Mr Shakespeare bit his lower lip and made a move to take me in his arms.

"Don't kiss me now," I said. "You will ruin my paint."

He laughed, Mr Shakespeare, my husband.

He threw back his head and he laughed, showing those two black broken teeth he'd got at the front. For once, it was as if he didn't mind me seeing them.

He gave me that peas porridge cloak, because it was raining.

"Keep it," said he. "I think it looks better on you."

It didn't.

But I thanked him for his kindness all the same.

I put on my hat and my gloves.

Mr Shakespeare reached for his lambskin jacket.

"It's all right, husband," I told him. "I will make my own way. You get on with your work now."

So he did.

And so did I.

And more's the pity.

Because that bed, now I come to look back on it, would have been plenty big enough to take the three of us.

Reader, I have told you of my husband, William Shakespeare.

And I have told you true, for I loved the man.

Now my story is almost ended, save for one word.

It was at his own end, in his final fever, just before he died in my arms, that my husband added a sentence between the lines of his last will and testament:

Item. I give unto my wife my second-best bed with the furniture.

Susanna says it is an insult.

I know otherwise.

What happened to that other bed, in every sense the best one?

If I knew, be sure, I would tell you, but I do not know.

I never dared ask Mr Shakespeare. And he never said.

Sometimes (before that bequest) I used to wake up in the night and wonder if I hadn't dreamt that bed, as well as what we did in it.

But now I know that if I did dream it, why, it must have been a dream Mr Shakespeare dreamt too.

*

My husband lies now seventeen feet deep in Trinity chancel beneath his own epitaph:

GOOD FRIEND, FOR JESU'S SAKE FORBEAR
TO DIG THE DUST ENCLOSED HERE:
BLEST BE THE MAN THAT SPARES THESE STONES,
AND CURST BE HE THAT MOVES MY BONES.

Rhymes which make it impossible, of course, for me to be buried with him when my own time comes.

Our mortal dust must lie separate, in different graves.

But this, as I told you, has been a love story, and ends so.

It is only on earth I shall sleep in the second-best bed.

Afterword

This is a work of fiction but it springs from William
Shakespeare's own writings and from the earliest writings
by others to take note of him – for instance, Robert
Greene's *Groatsworth of Wit* (1592) for the upstart crow;
Francis Meres' *Palladis Tamia, Wit's Treasury* (1598) for
the sweetness and the sugar; Nicholas Rowe's *Some
Account of the Life of Mr William Shakespeare* (1709) for
the gift of £1000 (quoting a story "handed down by Sir
William D'Avenant"); Samuel Johnson's 1765 preface to
the plays picking up another Davenant anecdote for the
horse-holding; the Revd John Ward (vicar of
Stratford-upon-Avon from 1662 to 1681) and an
anonymous correspondent collecting Warwickshire
gossip in the *British Magazine* (vol iii, 1762) for the
drinking; a note made by the Revd Richard Davies
(rector of Sapperton, Gloucestershire, 1695–1708) for the
dying a Papist; and so forth. The best modern biography
is S. Schoenbaum's *William Shakespeare: A
Documentary Life* (1975), which presents all the factual
evidence in documentary form. Regarding more
speculative matters (for example, Shakespeare's
blushing) I have allowed myself to make deductions
from the imagery of the poems and plays, and in this

particular instance I refer the reader also to Caroline Spurgeon's study *Shakespeare's Imagery and What It Tells Us* (1935). None of my sources can be held responsible for the central imaginative thesis of my book: that Anne Hathaway might have been the Dark Lady of the *Sonnets*.

Mrs Shakespeare: The Complete Works began life as a short story called "The Second Best Bed" which first appeared in an anthology entitled *Shakespeare Stories*, edited by Giles Gordon (Hamish Hamilton, 1982), and was then reprinted without change in my collection *The Facts of Life and Other Fictions* (Hamish Hamilton, 1983). I am grateful to Giles Gordon and to Christopher Sinclair-Stevenson for their interest in and encouragement of the work at every stage.

ROBERT NYE

Robert Nye was born in London in 1939. His principal calling is poetry, and his A COLLECTION OF POEMS 1955–1988 was chosen by six critics as one of their Books of the Year. His historical novels include FALSTAFF (winner of both the Hawthornden Prize and the *Guardian* Fiction Prize), MERLIN, FAUST, THE VOYAGE OF THE DESTINY, THE LIFE AND DEATH OF MY LORD GILLES DE RAIS, MRS SHAKESPEARE and, most recently, THE LATE MR SHAKESPEARE. His books have been translated into many languages, and he is also a respected literary journalist, having served for the past two decades as poetry critic for *The Times*.